Praise for
Hitchhiking with Larry David

"Like Larry David's TV shows, *Seinfeld* and *Curb Your Enthusiasm*, this curious memoir is witty, boasts an assortment of offbeat characters, and offers just a hint of surrealism. . . . A quirky and frequently thought-provoking memoir."
—***Booklist***

"Endearing and funny."   —***Martha's Vineyard Magazine***

"Light, witty, brave, and breezy, the perfect little book to stick in your beach bag this summer."   —**LifeGoesStrong.com**

"If I'd only known, I would've been wittier."
—**Larry David**, creator of
Seinfeld and *Curb Your Enthusiasm*

"Light, summery memoir of a journey toward healing from a relationship gone slightly sour."   —***Kirkus Reviews***

"Paul's wit, intelligence, and beautiful view of the world are all contained in this terrific read, and I believe it will inspire many to think about the potential everyone's thumb has to take them places beyond the complacent."
—*The Huffington Post*

"I should have picked him up. . . . Truly hysterical!"
—**David McCullough**, two-time
Pulitzer Prize winner and Martha's Vineyard resident

Paul Samuel Dolman, who now follows the mantra "you never know when magic will happen," has had many adventures in Martha's Vineyard, even though he lived with his parents. Dolman has dabbled in the film business in LA, founded a music company in Nashville, and is the author of the self-published book *What Matters Most*. He spends his summers on Martha's Vineyard and the rest of the year in Maui, Hawaii.

HITCHHIKING
WITH LARRY
DAVID

An Accidental Tourist's Summer
of Self-Discovery in Martha's Vineyard

PAUL SAMUEL DOLMAN

GOTHAM BOOKS

GOTHAM BOOKS
Published by the Penguin Group
Penguin Group (USA) LLC
375 Hudson Street
New York, New York 10014

USA | Canada | UK | Ireland | Australia | New Zealand | India | South Africa | China

penguin.com
A Penguin Random House Company

Previously published as a Gotham Books hardcover

First trade paperback printing, June 2014

10 9 8 7 6 5 4 3 2 1

Gotham Books and the skyscraper logo are trademarks of
Penguin Group (USA) LLC

The Library of Congress has cataloged the hardcover edition of this book as follows:
Dolman, Paul Samuel.
Hitchhiking with Larry David : an accidental tourist's summer of self-discovery in
Martha's Vineyard / Paul Samuel Dolman.
pages cm
ISBN 978-1-59240-826-9 (HC)   978-1-59240-874-0 (PBK)
1. Martha's Vineyard (Mass.)—Description and travel.   2. Dolman, Paul
Samuel—Travel—Massachusetts—Martha's Vineyard.   3. Dolman, Paul
Samuel—Childhood and youth.   4. Hitchhiking—Massachusetts—Martha's
Vineyard.   5. Dolman, Paul Samuel—Philosophy.   6. Self-actualization
(Psychology)   7. David, Larry.   8. Martha's Vineyard (Mass.)—Biography.
9. Martha's Vineyard (Mass.)—Social life and customs.   I. Title.
F72. M5D65 2013
917. 44'9404—dc23
2012047073

Printed in the United States of America
Set in Adobe Garamond • Designed by Spring Hoteling

*Penguin is committed to publishing works of quality and integrity.
In that spirit, we are proud to offer this book to our readers;
however, the story, the experiences, and the words are the author's alone.*

Contents

I believe in miracles.

For all the people throughout my life who have picked me up when I really needed a lift. Thank you!

Introduction

In the summer of 1974, Steven Spielberg and I landed on Martha's Vineyard. I came for a family vacation; he was there to shoot *Jaws*.

I stepped off the old, single-engine prop plane and knew instantly that this was where I belonged. Quite simply, it was love at first sight. I felt as if there were magic in the wind. My spine tingled; I could taste the sea on my lips. This place was home.

With its quaint New England charm and captivating beauty, the Vineyard sits off the base of Cape Cod, a mere seven miles from the reality of the mainland. With her pristine beaches and endless miles of green meadows, the island feels like heaven. There are no traffic lights, billboards, highways, or malls on this rock. An unguarded feeling permeates people's attitudes and tends to relax their faces. Yes, I know, an environment this laid-back and carefree sounds almost un-American. Which is precisely the charm of the place.

The island is cool in another way, too. While the rest of the country staggers through the sweltering heat of summer, the chilly Atlantic waters keep the Vineyard incubated in a comfortable climate with fragrant sea breezes. Even in the underbelly of August, it is not unusual to throw on a sweater when contemplating the stars.

Aside from the occasional "borrowed" bike, or the sight of me strolling along the nude beach, there is no real crime on these shores. The Vineyard is safe enough for residents to leave the front door open and the keys hanging in the ignition; even to do a little hitchhiking—sometimes with surprising results.

Both the world and I have changed quite a bit through the years, yet this magical little isle has managed to stay relatively unspoiled. Though I have traveled extensively, the Vineyard has always felt like home. It's the one place where I can completely let go and see the extraordinary in the ordinary.

CHAPTER 1

Soul Mates

At the age of forty-eight, feeling becalmed in listless waters without a following wind, I am drawn toward geographic salvation. I am once again on a plane returning to my summertime sanctuary, hopeful that my mystical island goddess can heal that which lies broken within me. I pray that the Vineyard's magic will repair not only some recent wounds, but maybe a few old ones, too.

God, has it really been six years since my last visit? There's no excuse for the lapse, other than wanting to avoid the insanity of my parents. Actually that's a pretty good reason. Visiting them in Florida during the winters has fulfilled my filial duties, up until now.

As the clouds pass below my wistful gaze, my mind drifts back a decade, to that time in Nashville, Tennessee, when I was running my company, South Beach

Entertainment, named for my place of birth. South Beach was more boutique than behemoth. The business allowed me to channel my love of music and empowering people into a career that was enjoyable, and eventually quite lucrative.

What did South Beach do? Whatever our clients needed or wanted. We helped songwriters to hone their image and select their songs; get their music to major artists; and get recorded. One client had a scenery company that built stages; another owned a recording studio in Florida that produced songs for television and film. We would pretty much do anything, as long as it was legal and somehow involved the most crucial aspect of any entertainment venture: long strategy sessions over ridiculously expensive dinners.

I had come to the Music City straight out of Berklee College of Music in Boston, the famous school where, for reasons that elude me to this day, I received a full scholarship to study composition and the piano. For two long years, I tiptoed around the hallowed halls, waiting for their expensive bookkeeping error to be discovered and for my deportation to commence. During that time, I also managed to write and record several songs that caught the attention of the Nashville publishing houses. After a few of the songs were actually published in exchange for a modest sum of money and a few pints of blood, I packed up my rat-infested Back Bay hovel and headed south.

I occupied my evenings playing piano at what was surely the world's smokiest bar. Not only did this place completely cure me of any stage fright, it also taught me to play a wide variety of show tunes while holding my breath for three to four hours at a time.

I also caught a break while pumping gas on my first full day in town. I noticed a guy across from me filling up his shiny ride, and figured since he had a new car and a beard, he had to be in the music industry. This calculation proved correct, and within a month I was working for his company in the tape room—the Nashville equivalent of the mailroom—making cassette tapes for the more successful writers in the firm. If it weren't for this one man, I would never have worked in the music business. And to this day, I have never forgiven him for it.

After about a year of this, I grew tired of earning close to minimum wage for making others wealthy, and I decided to hang my own shingle.

After a shaky start doing my own thing, I found my course, and my life slowly started to improve. It took a few years, with a little trial and a lot of error, but after a while my entertainment/consulting business began to kick out some pretty serious cash.

This seemed like a lot of fun, and I truly loved my mixed bag of talented clients. The challenges were difficult, but that made getting there all the more sweet. You had to be creative and immune to rejection—two qualities that would serve me well in so many other areas of my life. Over time, my clients became like an extended family, and I got a tremendous amount of joy watching them grow artistically. It was a thrill to see someone's lifelong dream become a reality, through hard work and determination. Much more important, doing this kind of thing kept me from having to work at a real job.

Of course with my newfound wealth, I did everything a Successful White Guy was supposed to do:

1) I bought a beautiful home in the woods, with lots of empty rooms.

2) I filled those rooms with expensive stuff made from Chinese slave labor.

3) I purchased an overpriced, high-end German car that was terrible for the environment.

4) I dated, supported, and lived with a stunning former supermodel who was dealing with substance abuse issues.

5) I put on some weight.

For the first couple of years, I was able to distract myself in a variety of ways, both healthy and unhealthy, from an ever-growing voice within that declared, *Something very important is missing that you desperately need to go discover.*

But what that "something" could be was the million-dollar question. Ironically, the more success I achieved, the louder the voice became. *Something very important is missing that you desperately need to go discover.*

But what about all the money that was flowing in every week? Was I supposed to just walk away from it all? Wasn't that against the law in America?

You have more than enough. Let it all go, and go find yourself!

The house, the cars, the cash, and the crazy girlfriend, I should give all that up? After all that ~~ass-kissing~~ work I had to do to get them?

You have more than enough. Let it all go, and go find yourself!

That's easy for you to say; you're a disembodied voice that doesn't need to eat, or have a steady regimen of image-reinforcing, yet somehow shallow sex. I could end up living in a cardboard box behind Walmart or, even worse, with my parents.

You have more than enough. Let it all go, and go find yourself!

Oy!

Somehow, some way, I found the courage to do just that. I let it all go. It took a couple of years, and in the interim my ego tried to move the whole show to the Los Angeles film industry, but ultimately I shut down the company and began to try to figure out what I really wanted to do with my life.

I made temporary forays into several new areas. First, I launched a motivational speaking career. The practical upside was obvious: Someone was paying me to talk, as opposed to what I had grown used to: people paying me to shut up. That went quite well until one day I suddenly realized that I had absolutely no idea what the hell I was talking about.

Then I attempted a few screenplays. Next, I embraced a grand vision to help save the world that fared only slightly better than the *Hindenburg*. I also did a whole lot of traveling, but nothing was saying, *This is it!*

Then I met a girl . . .

It's the day after Christmas in sunny Del Mar. I have come here on a whim, at the invitation of an old friend. Having exited all external responsibilities in Nashville, it was also a wonderful alternative to another gray, dreary December in Tennessee. The plan was to take a week or two walking the beach here, before heading even farther west to see some friends in Hawaii.

It is a picture-perfect postcard day. A friend arrives from Los Angeles with the well-known spiritual author Dick Sutphen, writer of the bestselling book *Soul Agreements*. The three of us share the day and discuss, among other things, the mysterious topic of soul mates.

DICK'S WELLSPRING OF WISDOM

Do soul mates really exist? Yes, most certainly.

Do we have only one in a lifetime? Not necessarily.

How do we find them? Follow your heart.

How will we know when we meet them? Trust me, you will know.

Does love between souls transcend death? Absolutely.

I describe what has been happening in my life recently, and Dick says, "It sounds as though you may soon meet your soul mate."

"Well, it's going to take a miracle for that to happen," I reply sarcastically.

The next day I get a call from a woman whom I met on Myspace, inviting me for tea. An hour later, I walk down the block and meet her at a seaside café. After a few minutes of chatting, she suddenly insists, "You have to meet my roommate. I feel like you two would really connect. I'm picking her up from the airport tonight, and she's leaving for Aspen in the morning, so it has to be this evening. How about I call my boyfriend, and the four of us have dinner?"

Feeling as if I should be open to the idea, I agree, and Ms. Myspace drives off.

An hour later, the three of them walk through my door. The roommate is stunningly beautiful, with olive skin, green eyes, flowing sun-streaked hair, and a smile that could melt a wall of ice. Yet, oddly, she lacks the pretense that usually accompanies such a stunning storefront.

I love the sound of her voice; the resonant tones, the calming phrases, and the careful consideration of her words. We finish each other's sentences and share a common worldview. This woman seems to totally get me, see me, and feel me.

As we are preparing the meal, our eyes connect, allowing me to witness an even greater beauty within. She encompasses a depth, compassion, softness, and sensitivity unlike anything I have experienced. An inexplicable familiarity exists between us that we openly acknowledge. Crossing paths in the kitchen, we spontaneously embrace.

I can't help myself; I say, "Holding you feels like coming home."

She blushes.

Who is this person? Why do I feel as if I already know her? What is happening here?

We enjoy a delicious dinner of Pasta Paul-ivera, and then settle into a long, interesting conversation. Near midnight I say to the beautiful roommate, "This is great, but don't you need to go home and sleep? Otherwise, you'll be exhausted for your ski trip."

"Oh, I decided not to go. On the flight back home I was reading this fascinating book called *Soul Agreements,* and it changed my perspective on dating. I've decided not to waste any more time, and wait for the real thing instead."

"What?" I nearly fall off the couch. I mean, of all the books in the world to mention! "I spent yesterday with the author in this very room, discussing soul mates!"

She is just as astounded as I am.

The next day we decide to take a local yoga class, and as we are signing in I see that her surname happens to be . . . Miracle!

"Miracle? That's your last name? No one told me that was your last name. That's *not* your last name."

She smiles.

"Really?" I say, incredulous.

"Since the day I was born."

Hmmm . . . this is getting interesting.

After our class, we go for a long walk on the beach, and for the first time I take her hand in mine. The day turns into night, and before long, fourteen hours have flown by.

Before she leaves, I ask, "Can I show you a recent entry in my journal?" She nods. "Here, look at this: 'It's going to take a miracle for me to find someone to share my soul with.' I had no idea my words would be taken so literally."

She laughs and adds, "This is getting interesting . . ."

As she pulls out of the driveway, I realize that I already miss her. Something beautiful is happening.

The next day, a highly intuitive friend pulls me aside and says of the Miracle, "I'm not saying she is the one—but she's the one."

Instead of leaving after ten days as planned, I decide to stay at my friend's gigantic beach house in Del Mar. Two weeks turns into two months, in what feels like two minutes. During that time, the Miracle and I spend every minute together, and at my behest she returns home to Nashville with me.

Over the next two years, we spent our days discovering each other again for the first time. Unfortunately, after that auspicious beginning and a wonderful middle, we drifted into the relationship rapids and started taking on more and more water. Our troubles seemed to feed off one another, and I began to have major doubts about whether we were right for each other. My reluctance to commit only triggered her abandonment issues, which set off her defenses and caused her to act out. Which activated my fears of commitment, which then ignited . . . You get the idea.

By this point, we literally could not get along or agree

on anything. If our relationship were a book, it would have been called *The Four Disagreements:*

1) Never Tell the Truth.

2) Take Everything Personally.

3) Make Wild Assumptions.

4) Do Everything Half-Assed.

It reached a low point where she finally moved out and started dating another guy, but not without returning for spontaneous overnight visits on a regular basis.

If that sounds like Love Limbo Hell, you're right.

Feeling panicked, I had to do something, so once again I reached out to my enchanted isle in the hope of salvation. Was it just me grasping at straws, or was some strong force pulling me back to the Vineyard? I wasn't sure, but in the end I decided to just go with it.

I had several choices. I could rent a very small house in Edgartown—thus spending thousands of dollars I really didn't have anymore since listening to the financially irresponsible disembodied voice. I could stay with my parents in an updated version of the Bates Motel. Or, I could camp in the woods like the Unabomber, and be covered with ticks. Believe it or not, I almost chose the ticks.

Try as I might to spin this thing, it looked, on paper, like I was merely trading one form of suffering for another. But after a few more heartbreaking episodes with the Miracle, I decided to take my chances and head toward the

Vineyard. Besides, maybe this was the summer my parents would finally come to their senses and realize what a wonderful son they had.*

With both my ability to sleep and my appetite rapidly evaporating, I threw some clothes into a bag and hopped on a plane to Martha's Vineyard. The game plan was to catch my spiritual breath, avoid contact with the Miracle, and try to figure out what the hell had happened to my life.

---

* Yes, I know this sentence is reminiscent of every alien invasion film ever made, where the small-town farm folk approach the dangerous-looking creatures and say, "Hey, I bet these critters are friendly."

CHAPTER 2

The Parental Asylum

It all started thirty-five years ago, when my parents bought some land in the woods of outer Edgartown. For years they scrimped, saved, clipped coupons, cut corners, and fought like mad to build a place for themselves. Just to be clear, I should point out that all of the combat was waged exclusively against each other. Mom was the driving force behind the construction, while Dad was *unofficially* against the project. He instituted a campaign of passive resistance that Gandhi himself would have envied. But to be fair to my father, his default setting sits perpetually at "no." In other words, he's pretty much against any initiative that requires him to leave his seat.

Every summer, my parents migrate by wagon train from Saint Augustine, Florida, to this tiny cabin in Martha's Vineyard that I fondly call The Parental Asylum.

When visiting them, you never know what to expect. It could be peaceful for a brief interlude (we're talking three days max), or a harrowing hellhole (stay for anything longer than a week, and you have only yourself to blame). You might be welcome (Mom), or you might not (Dad). Through the years, their roles have become well defined: Mom invites you to stay as long as you'd like, while Dad makes you feel as if it's time for you to move on by the end of the first day.

The fact is, Dad only has the social energy to be nice to humans for about ten minutes a day. This allotment of pleasantries is usually exhausted at the supermarket, or on the phone with a customer service representative, trying to save a few bucks through some once-in-a-lifetime offer.

The Parental Asylum sits nestled at the dead end of a dirt road, so there's never much traffic. With its cedar walls, the place is rustic and down-home. Mom's choice of decorating motif? Early American Cluttered. Every available space, from counters to walls, is covered in a variety of garage sale knick-knacks, such as: a General Robert E. Lee Memorial Tea Set, a tattered map of Armenia, a list of *Reader's Digest* Top Ten Jigsaw Puzzles, and old publicity stills of Clark Gable.

My bags not yet unpacked, I take a quick visual tour of the house. Though much of the decor could spark a lively debate, I focus on one piece that is particularly puzzling. I point to what looks like an old ice pick. "Hey, Mom, what's this?"

"Oh, be careful with that," she says. "I bought it a couple of years ago at the bishop's garage sale. It's a Pope Pius the Twelfth pickax."

All of this junk is thrown together in the same way that birds tend to grab anything available when building a nest. Mom's designing mantra is *Let no space go unused*. It would take a Stephen Hawking to find any rhyme or reason to all this decorative chaos.

Truth has always been elusive in our family, with the level of veracity hovering just below the old Soviet newspaper *Pravda*. For example, despite constant claims to the contrary, Mom and Dad spend most of their time in front of the television. They prefer old films, reruns, and news programs warning them of impending doom. Every Sunday night they watch *60 Minutes,* then PBS; on Tuesdays, it's always Animal Planet. In fact, their entire schedule, whether TV programming or food consumption, is pretty much set in stone. What works best is to never ask them to step outside their shared comfort zone.

THE FIVE DEADLY QUESTIONS
Does anyone want to . . .

visit Edgartown?

watch the sunset?

go somewhere?

go anywhere?

change the routine in any conceivable way?

Mom has even written out the summer breakfast schedule and posted it on the refrigerator: Monday: eggs . . .

Tuesday: bagels . . . Wednesday . . . You get the idea. As a practical joke, I considered rearranging and reprinting the schedule, *just to see what would happen.*

My parents' miniature dachshund, Max, is the last member of our strange aggregation. Max has the dubious honor of being the only carbon-based life-form my parents feel comfortable having around, despite the fact that he barks at anything and everything that moves. Lately, in an effort to shake things up around the house, Max has added to his repertoire things that *don't* move. This is Mom's cue to say in a stern voice, "No barking, Max." Five minutes later, he's back at it again, followed by the familiar refrain: "No barking!" Since this pattern of futility has gone on consistently for ten years, I'm going to go out on a limb here and suggest that Max doesn't seem to get it.

One of Max's annual rituals is getting skunked. I guess he hasn't figured that one out, either. I wouldn't want to call Max dumb, but he's not the sharpest pup in the litter. Through extensive, hands-on research, we've discovered that he only knows two words:

1) his name

2) and another word—we just haven't quite figured out what it is yet.

For some bewildering reason, every time I reach for Max, one of my parents will say, "Don't hurt him." Having never harmed an animal in my life, nor even entertained such an unfathomable notion, I can't figure out why my actions provoke these repeated warnings. Upon reflection, I conclude that this phrase must be some kind of unique blessing bestowed upon the breed. So, in an effort to fit in, every time one of them touches Max, I also say, "Don't hurt him."

This always elicits a bewildered look from them, and the comment, "We would *never* hurt Max!"

CHAPTER 3

We Make Contact

I cope with my parents' eccentricities by spending most of my time away from the Asylum. On a typical day, I bicycle for hours, swim in the chilly waters of the Atlantic, and hitchhike around the island. Yes, I could get around solely on my bike, by public transportation, or with my parents' car, but I would miss out on countless fascinating encounters. And so, I stick out my thumb.

After years of hitching on this island, I have become familiar with the tenets of its unwritten code, which I will share with you now:

The Official MVY Hitchhiker's Manifesto

Stand up straight and keep your hands out of your pockets. No shades or hats, and you'd better not have a backpack (it could have a bomb in it). Smile a lot—sincerely if possible; insincerely if hung over. And clean is always better than filthy.

It's easier for one person to get a ride than two, unless you're with a woman. An obvious rule of thumb: The prettier the girl, the faster the ride (just as in life). A gorgeous woman alone will get a ride immediately, and if she's seriously hot, she might cause a major pileup. Trying to hitch with three people is extremely difficult, and with a group of guys wearing turbans, it's next to impossible.

It's much harder to hitch with a dog, unless it's a puppy or a yellow Lab. Stay away from farm livestock or, God forbid, any creature that appears to be rabid or what is traditionally considered a wild animal (i.e., lions, bears, cobras, et cetera).

Your best times of operation are during the daylight hours. It's very challenging at night, at least until the bars get out—but then you run the risk of getting into a car with a drunken maniac. Being maimed or crippled in a bad accident would likely put a damper on your summer.

After being picked up, politely attempt some kind of conversation with the occupants and, based on the response, take your cue from there. Any mumbling, hitting, or biting by the driver is a sign to keep quiet for the remainder of the trip.

The older the driver, the less likely the ride. "Those lazy kids should walk like we used to. The world is going to hell, I tell you!" Yet older cars stop more frequently than newer ones; especially old Volvos. (Save the whales!) Convertibles, classic cars, and Jeeps with no tops tend to stop a lot. Yuppies in SUVs, repairmen, commercial vans, motorcycles, police vehicles, tour buses, ice cream trucks, and tractors almost never do.

Lastly, it is bad form to flip people off if they pass you by. This rule applies no matter how long you have been standing in the rain while being eaten alive by mosquitoes. As in life, it's best not to take the rejection personally.

With the sun on my face, I stand by the side of the road, small bag of pastries from the dougÚut shop in hand, for my first official hitch of the season. I'm off to a rocky start; there's been no action for the past half hour. Although discouraged, I quickly bounce back and comfort myself with the mantra, *Not to worry; the perfect car will pick me up.* Maybe the lessons of *The Secret* really do work—although I must admit to being skeptical ever since I heard about some New Age place in California called The Prosperity Center going out of business. I decide to give it another try and begin to visualize . . . a vintage car filled with Swedish nannies who are headed to the beach for a little fun. They've packed a gourmet lunch that they wish to share with me, along with their company.

A car approaches (okay, here we go) . . . My thumb goes out . . . No sign of blond hair (no problem, I'm not picky) . . . It looks like an older guy (maybe he's just the nannies' driver) . . . He's slowing down (spirits sinking a bit) . . . No nannies (falling lower) . . . The guy is balding, with glasses (completely deflated) . . .

But wait—I recognize this guy from pictures in magazines. In fact, didn't I just read some brilliant piece written by him in *The New York Times*? Yes, somehow my nascent psychic powers have manifested the actor, comedian, writer, and fellow *Homo sapien,** Larry David.

Cut to . . .

(Car pulls over)

> **Larry David:** Need a ride?

> **Hitchhiker:** Yes. Thank you.

As I get into the car, Larry looks at me suspiciously, with eyebrows raised. He's contorting his body away from me as his hands firmly grasp the steering wheel.

> **Larry:** Umm . . . You're not a serial killer or something, are you?

A reasonable enough request, but one extended with funky timing. If he was seriously concerned for his life, he should have asked me this *before* I got into the car. Not wishing to further startle my host organism, I take a few moments to consider my reply.

---

* Attorney's note: *Homo sapiens,* or humans, are bipedal primates in the family Hominidae. This reference is in no way meant as a commentary on Mr. David's sexual preference.

Hitchhiker: Well, Larry, it's the summer and we are on the Vineyard. So even if I was, I'm on vacation and not working.

Larry laughs; the ticking-bomb tension has been defused. He sticks out his hand, and we shake. Larry is wearing casual attire—a light short-sleeved shirt and khaki pants. I'm in an old weathered T-shirt and shorts.

Larry: That's good enough for me. Where are you going?

Hitchhiker: To be honest, I'm not really sure. How about Aquinnah?

This is asking a lot of my new driver. It's a good fifteen miles from here to the very tip of the island. The roads are long and winding, and I figured it would take me at least two or three rides to make it all the way there. So if Larry agrees, I will have the luxury of one constant companion the whole way. Unfortunately, my request has shocked him.

Cut to . . .

(Larry jolts backward.)

Larry: That's the farthest point of the island!

Hitchhiker: Hey, take me as far as you like. I can always get another ride.

What's the old adage, beggars and hitchhikers can't be choosy?

Larry (thinking about it for a minute): Well, why the hell not.

Hitchhiker: Really?

I can't believe my good fortune.

Larry: It's a beautiful day. Let's go.

It truly is the most stunning of days. I look out the windshield at an endless blue sky with a few cumulus clouds hanging around as if they had nothing better to do. The humidity has taken a day off, so the late-June air is unusually crisp. The windows are wide open, offering us a refreshing sea breeze as we ride along in silence. After a few moments, Larry breaks the ice.

Larry: You know, I never pick up hitchhikers.

Hitchhiker: Really?

Larry: Really.

Hitchhiker: How come?

Larry (grimacing a little): Well, it's usually a bit awkward, and you never know what or who you're going to encounter.

Hitchhiker: So you've never picked anyone up before?

Larry: I once stopped to pick up a girl, and then there was this creepy-looking guy standing behind the bushes waiting to jump out and get in, too. So I just quickly drove away.

Hitchhiker: They tried to pull the old hitch-hiking double cross.

Larry (turning toward me and smiling): Is that what they call it?

Hitchhiker: It's a trick a lot of amateurs use. That's something a pro would never try.

Larry: Have you ever pulled that one?

Hitchhiker: A few times early in my career. Maybe when I was with a girlfriend and we were stuck out in the boonies late at night, when it's almost impossible to get a ride. But no one ever drove off like you did.

Larry (defensively): I was surprised; it felt a little tricky.

Hitchhiker: Most of the time when that happens to the driver, they are pretty pissed off. So the ride can be weird and awkward.

Larry: Is this hitchhiking thing something you do a lot?

Hitchhiker (thinking about it for a second): God, I haven't hitchhiked in years. Today was the first time in I don't know how long that I've stuck out my thumb.

Larry: Lucky me . . .

Hitchhiker: Yesterday I rode my bike for about forty miles, and now my legs are killing me. I promised some friends I would meet them up at the beach in Aquinnah, so I had no choice. I had to stick out the old thumb.

Larry: Don't you have a car?

Hitchhiker: I could use my parents' car, but my father probably wouldn't like that. In fact, he's not too crazy about me even being here.

Larry (surprised): You're living at home?

Hitchhiker: No, just visiting indefinitely . . .

Larry laughs.

Hitchhiker: I'm probably only staying a week or two. I'm sure my dad will run me off after that.

Larry: So the old guy is pretty tough?

Hitchhiker: He wasn't always like that, but man, the last thirty years . . .

Larry (smiling): So you went hitchhiking . . . and I picked you up, even though I never pick anyone up.

Hitchhiker: Then why did you pick up me?

Larry doesn't answer for a moment or two; he just stares ahead as we wend our way slowly up-island. We are passing golden pastoral fields of various crops, with the occasional grazing livestock. Just when I think he is not going to answer, he says,

> **Larry:** I really don't know; I just felt like I was supposed to.
>
> **Hitchhiker:** That's pretty deep.
>
> **Larry (sternly):** Now, don't get too heavy on me; we still have a long way to go here.

I hold up my hands like a bank robber caught in the act. The last thing I want to do is offend my host and get kicked out of the car five minutes into the ride.

> **Larry:** By the way, are you Jewish?
>
> **Hitchhiker:** Are you?

Larry shoots me a look that says, *Are you kidding?*

> **Hitchhiker:** I think my actual lineage is mongrel.
>
> **Larry:** Mongrel, huh.
>
> **Hitchhiker:** My mom is a disenchanted Irish Catholic, and Dad's lineage is all over the map—Germany, Austria, Odessa, Russia . . . When I look up my family tree, most of my recent ancestors still have tails. Actually Mom grew up in

Queens; Dad was from Brooklyn, and yes, his heritage is Jewish.

This seems to strike a chord in Larry, and he becomes a bit more animated.

Larry: Jewish? Brooklyn?

Hitchhiker: Yes . . .

Larry: That's where I was born. Do you know where he grew up?

Hitchhiker: I think it was very close to Ebbets Field.

Larry: I grew up in Sheepshead Bay. Was he a fan of the old Brooklyn Dodgers?

Hitchhiker: He lived and died with them.

For a moment my mind drifts back to when I was ten and my father and I stayed up late listening to Larry King on the radio. King was interviewing a host of people about what life was like growing up in Brooklyn. The guests spoke of the Dodgers, interesting food, etÚic boundaries, and what life was like pre– and post–World War II. Later, in a rare moment of intimacy, my dad filled in some details about his life, providing my first glimpse of what his childhood was like.

Larry's voice brings me back to the present.

Larry: God, those were wonderful days. Did you and your dad talk about those times much?

Hitchhiker: We used to be able to connect, but as I got older that connection was lost . . .

Larry: That can be a generational thing, you know.

(There is a moment of quiet, and then he goes in a new direction.)

Do you live in New York?

Hitchhiker: No, Nashville.

Larry (cocking his head): You don't strike me as a Nashville guy. No *you alls* . . . Did you grow up in the South, and how did you end up here?

Hitchhiker: Actually, yes and no. I grew up in South Florida, but we spent some vacations here at the Vineyard when I was a kid. Later on, I started coming here and getting summer jobs doing a variety of things. I worked in a bike store, I drove a cab, and for years I played the piano. After college in Boston, I moved to Nashville, where they considered my Florida birthplace and declared me a Yankee; I had to get out an atlas to make sure I hadn't missed something . . .

Larry (considering me): You should live in New York.

Hitchhiker: I should?

Larry: Yes, you should.

Hitchhiker: Big cities have always felt tough for me. The energy is great, but I need more trees than concrete. And there's not enough sun.

Larry: I'm thinking New York would be good for you.

Hitchhiker (laughing): Okay, I'll have to check into that. Speaking of trees, isn't this place beautiful? Look at these rolling hills.

We are cruising up the South Road, and have just passed the sign letting us know that we are entering Chilmark. There are no commercial structures on either side of the road; only flowing fields and crumbling stone walls. We pass crooked mailboxes bearing hand-painted names. Some of those names strike a chord of familiarity for me. One Vineyard summer years ago, I worked as a taxi driver and was fortunate enough to navigate many of these dirt and gravel roads. Often they led to hidden estates with glorious views, private beaches that were hard to reach, or dilapidated farmhouses with indifferent livestock dotting the pastures.

Larry: I love it here.

Hitchhiker: It is easy to love. How long do you stay?

Larry: I try to stay the whole summer, though I have to leave now and again. My kids are here, so it works out well. I have two daughters, and they have their jobs and friends, so it's a good place for us to spend time together.

Hitchhiker: Do you love being a dad?

Larry: You know, you ask an awful lot of questions.

Hitchhiker: I guess I'm just curious.

Larry: That's a nice way to put it. But yes, I really do enjoy being a father. It's a lot more fun now that they are older, and they're these wonderful people you love to be around.

Hitchhiker: I imagine they grow up fast.

Larry: You have no idea.

It seems like only a few short years ago that I was a young boy riding my bike through Edgartown with a fishing rod, my younger brother, Chris, trailing behind me. We'd head to the wharf to try our luck with live bait from the old tackle shop. We always made a stop at the little candy store to stock up on sweets, which helped distract us from the lack of action on the other end of the line. Which was fine since I was never really comfortable with the poor fish getting a hook in his mouth. I was more than happy just to watch the sailboats come and go while feasting on Smarties and Orange Slices.

Hitchhiker: What do you do here all summer?

Larry: Work on my show, play some golf, and see my kids . . . What about you?

Hitchhiker: Ride my bike, eat a lot, swim, write in my journal.

Larry: Are you a writer?

Hitchhiker: I write stuff down, but I've never really written anything substantial. I published a book once called *What Matters Most,* which was a collection of interviews with people.

Larry (nodding and smiling): So you like to ask a lot of questions. I see a disturbing trend here.

Hitchhiker: You got me. Do you write every day?

Larry: No, because on my show I wear several hats. I have to divide up the time between writing and the other stuff.

Hitchhiker: Do you love to write?

Larry takes a few moments with this one, then gives a slight grimace.

Larry: I wouldn't say that. It's a lot of work.

It strikes me that he is being remarkably honest, straightforward, and easygoing about all of this. Here is this guy who's pretty famous, sharing personal stuff with some middle-aged guy he picked up hitchhiking. The thought makes me want to give him something in return. I reach into my backpack, and Larry glances at me.

> **Hitchhiker:** This is where I pull out the gun . . . (I pull out my bag of broken pastries.) Would you like one of these dougåuts?
>
> **Larry (making a face):** I think I'll pass.

I realize that earlier this morning I had inadvertently chosen a cheese Danish, one of the Miracle's favorite pastries; this whisks me back to a wonderfully romantic morning in Del Mar. Conversing intimately in a tiny café overlooking the mighty Pacific, we shared one of these tasty treats while sipping cups of aromatic dark Colombian brew. Good Lord, what a memory.

> **Hitchhiker:** Larry, have you ever felt lost?
>
> **Larry:** Yes, of course.
>
> **Hitchhiker:** I feel like I've somehow ended up off the beaten path.
>
> **Larry:** That's not always a bad thing.
>
> **Hitchhiker:** No?
>
> **Larry:** Sometimes you have to wander a bit, and do what you don't want to in order to figure out what it is you're supposed to do. What brought you here?

Hitchhiker: If I'm honest, I'm trying to get over a girl.

Larry gives me an empathetic look.

Hitchhiker: It was this beautiful thing, we struggled a lot and it turned sour, and then in the end we simply crashed and burned . . . It's been tough.

Larry (nodding, a serious look on his face): Were you married?

Hitchhiker: No. I thought about it with her, but was afraid to commit. I wasn't sure . . .

Larry: Did she drop you?

How much detail do I go into? I've been wearing my friends out with this stuff for the last couple of months; when you go through a tough breakup, your buddies bear the burden of the crisis: the back-and-forth, the ins and outs, the endless processing—hell, I'm sick of me talking about it. So I decide to give Larry a break and keep it brief.

Hitchhiker: It kind of just drifted and descended until it crashed. It was terrible; I haven't been able to sort it all out yet. I thought being on the Vineyard would help.

Larry: Well, it can't hurt.

Hitchhiker: (I gaze out the window for a moment or two.)

No, it can't. Hey, thanks for asking.

Larry: I'm sorry.

Hitchhiker: I appreciate that. Perhaps some space will help us.

Larry: Relationships are tough.

Hitchhiker: Are you married?

Larry: No, divorced.

Hitchhiker: Oh, I'm sorry.

Larry: It's been a couple of years. The hardest part is over.

Hitchhiker: The beginning is the worst.

Larry: Yes, it is.

We pass a gray-haired guy in a Jeep who looks a lot like the actor Ted Danson. Since Ted and his wife, Mary, live up here, I assume it was him.

Hitchhiker: Do you know Ted Danson?

Larry: Yes, he's a very good friend. He's been on my show, too. Have you seen it?

Hitchhiker: The show, or the one with Ted?

Larry: Either.

The moment I recognized Larry, I had a fleeting feeling of panic when I realized that I'd never seen a single episode of either of his shows. But my fears subsided when I considered the odds of its coming up. Unfortunately, it looks like I was wrong.

Hitchhiker: Uh, well . . . No, I can't say I ever have . . . ever seen that one with Ted.

Larry (sensing something): But you *have* seen the show, right?

Hitchhiker: Um . . . which one?

Larry: Either one. You've seen . . . Wait a minute . . .

Hitchhiker (uh-oh . . . this isn't good): Okay, first of all, I am not a TV guy.

Larry: You mean . . .

Hitchhiker (realizing I'm busted): I'm probably one of five people on the planet who hasn't seen *Seinfeld*.

Larry: What?

Hitchhiker: And no, I haven't seen your new one, either.

Larry: My *new* one? The "new" one is about to start its seventh season!

Hitchhiker: Oh? (I pause.) Congratulations!

Larry: Are you saying you have never seen *either* of my shows? Not even *Seinfeld*?

Hitchhiker: Don't take it personally. I told you, I'm not a television guy. I get all my culture from books and magazines.

Larry: Now, wait . . . Do you watch movies?

Hitchhiker: Of course. I love films.

Larry: Do you rent DVDs?

Hitchhiker: Yes, I rent DVDs.

Larry: Then why not get my shows on DVD?

Hitchhiker: I guess I could do that.

Larry (grinning): After all, why would you deny yourself so much pleasure?

Hitchhiker: Okay, you win. I'll tell you what: I'll watch your show in exchange for this ride. Deal?

Larry: Okay then, we have a deal.

I hold out my hand, and we shake.

Hitchhiker: Here's some irony for you. I can't get my parents to watch the sunset because they'd rather watch your reruns.

Larry: Really?

Hitchhiker: Yes, they pass on the sunset.

Larry: Well . . . seen one, seen 'em all . . .

I look out my window past the Allen Farm's rambling fields to the sparkling Atlantic Ocean. The water is brilliant with the reflection of the sun's rays.

>**Hitchhiker:** But you have to enjoy the island's natural beauty.
>
>**Larry:** In a way—but no, not really. (He smiles, and I can see a joke coming.) I need to be on drugs to connect with nature.
>
>**Hitchhiker:** That is really funny.

Since he seems so open, I decide to ask him one of my all-time favorite questions.

>**Hitchhiker:** Do you believe in fate?
>
>**Larry:** Not really. Do you?
>
>**Hitchhiker:** Sometimes. Certain things have happened in my life that seem—how do I say it? Like they were very well orchestrated. Do you know what I mean?
>
>**Larry:** Yes, but there's no way to explain it. I do believe in luck.
>
>**Hitchhiker:** Even this ride . . .
>
>**Larry:** Well, we all make mistakes.
>
>**Hitchhiker (laughing):** By the way, I really appreciate the ride.

Larry: Don't mention it. I didn't realize I was going to be interviewed, but it's been fun.

Since we seem to be in a flow, I open up the conversational grab bag to ask if he believes in one of our big cultural myths.

Hitchhiker: Can money buy you happiness?

Larry: No. (He pauses for a moment.) But it's better to have it, than not. Money can't make you happy, but it can make you happier.

Hitchhiker: What's it feel like to have a lot of money?

Larry: Funny, most days I don't even think about it.

Since most of us are obsessed with monetary thinking—*I need more, how do I keep it, what should I save, how much does it cost, who needs some of mine, do I have enough*—his answer sort of surprises me.

Hitchhiker: Did success help make you happy?

Larry: Who said I was happy?

Hitchhiker: That was a good one. Why do you think you were successful?

Larry: I got lucky. I found a partner that the public happened to like.

Hitchhiker: Was that Jerry?

Larry: Yes. He was the perfect person to relay my brand of comedy. I'm not sure I would have had the success I had without that connection.

Hitchhiker: So luck was huge.

Larry: Luck always plays a part for everyone, whether they want to admit it or not. I was very lucky, and I know it.

Hitchhiker: What brings you the most satisfaction?

Larry: Let me think about that for a moment . . . That's a tough one . . . I guess it's when I discover a really great idea and start developing it.

Hitchhiker: That's number one?

Larry (thinking for a moment): And making a woman laugh. (He pauses.) What is that about?

Hitchhiker: I like that, too . . .

Larry: And the prettier the woman, the more satisfaction I get. It doesn't make any sense, but I'm being honest.

Hitchhiker: It probably goes back to the caveman comedians, where only the funny would survive. I mean, think about it—it certainly gives a whole new meaning to dying onstage. By the way, what's it like to make it really big?

Larry: Who said I made it big?

Hitchhiker: That's true, it's only television.

Larry: Very funny, smart guy. Remember, you still have a very long way to Aquinnah if the ride ends here.

Hitchhiker: Seriously, though . . .

Larry: The whole process is a hard thing to describe. To me, it feels kind of surreal.

Hitchhiker: Even after all this time?

Larry (nodding): I'm not sure it ever completely sinks in. And so much changes, and yet nothing really does . . . You would like to think that you don't change, but I am sure in a lot of ways, you do.

I take a few moments to process this, and then I decide to ask another question.

Hitchhiker: What drove you to be successful?

Larry: I had to follow my dream. I couldn't continue working in a job I hated. So whatever it took to make it, obviously within the law, I was willing to do.

Hitchhiker: That was courageous.

Larry: Not really, because I had no choice. I had to do this, or I would die.

I think about my own jumble of dreams and ambitions. Right now everything seems upside down and out of sorts; my best-laid plans have been put aside, along with all that I'd projected for myself. Maybe taking time off this summer will help put me back on track.

> **Hitchhiker:** Wow, this is really a magical ride.
>
> **Larry (laughing):** Maybe for you.

We pass the old Chilmark Store with its faded front porch strewn with rocking chairs, people mingling about. This is an excellent spot for pizza, especially after spending the morning up the road at Lucy Vincent Beach.

> **Hitchhiker (motioning toward the store):** Hey, why don't we have lunch sometime? My treat.
>
> **Larry: (He looks at the store, then back at me. Considers the request for a moment, and then . . .)** No.

Well, I had to try.

> **Larry:** Hey, wait a minute; you claim you've never seen my program. Right?
>
> **Hitchhiker:** That's true, but I plan to catch up with that before the summer ends.
>
> **Larry:** Because we made a deal . . . But how did you know who I was?

Hitchhiker: I've seen your picture in magazines and on websites. You did a great thing in *The New York Times* recently that was hysterical.

Larry (seeming genuinely pleased): Thank you.

Hitchhiker: I love the way you write. Also, along with my parents, my younger brother, Chris, is a huge fan of your new show.

Larry: *Curb Your Enthusiasm.*

Hitchhiker: Yes. He's been telling me to watch it for years.

Larry: It's a lot of work to put something together. People have no idea how much energy and time is involved.

We have now entered Aquinnah; our last few minutes are at hand. I'm smiling inside at the fact that we had such a nice connection. What a crazy world. I know our paths will probably never cross again, but for this little piece of time, we shared something. The car crests a hill, and we come upon a stunning overlook of Menemsha Pond. It appears like something out of a postcard, with its tiny sailboats moored in the deep blue water. This is the first time in a while that I have been up-island, and the beauty of it never ceases to take my breath away. This feeling inspires me to ask one last question.

Hitchhiker: Here's one for you: Do you believe in a higher power or universal intelligence?

Larry (taking a moment to consider): Oh God, yes! I mean, you have to believe in something higher and wiser. Especially when you look at this . . . (He makes a sweeping gesture toward the heavens.) I mean, look at all this.

Hitchhiker: It's so miraculous.

Larry: And how perfect it is. (He shakes his head.) I'm not sure what *it* is, but there's definitely something.

Hitchhiker: What do you think matters most?

Larry: That is a really big question. (He thinks for a while.) Being true to yourself and doing whatever it is that you really have to do. I'm talking about the thing you love to do, in your one and only life . . . You have to do that.

Hitchhiker: Following your dream.

Larry: You have to do that.

Well, here we are at the end of the line. Larry pulls over to let me out. I gather my backpack.

Hitchhiker: Thank you. Hey, I still think we should go to lunch.

Larry (laughing): Absolutely not! Now get out of here. Who knows, I'll probably see you around.

Hitchhiker: I hope so. Again, thank you. I really enjoyed the ride.

Larry: Me too.

(He shakes my hand.)

Now get out.

I do, and with that Larry turns around, waves goodbye, and drives off.

CHAPTER 4

The Gospel of *Seinfeld*

Larry David created the television show *Seinfeld*. You may have heard of it. It was such a highly commercial, critical favorite that *TV Guide* named it the greatest television program of all time. *Seinfeld* was on the air for nine years, and is considered by many to be a cultural phenomenon. Yet all of this was somehow accomplished without my viewing a single episode. Go figure.

My parents, however, make up for my *Seinfeld*-viewing delinquency by watching the reruns religiously. (There is a scientific explanation for all this: Researchers believe the television-watching gene tends to skip a generation.)

Tonight is no exception, as I return home to find them entrenched in *Seinfeld* heaven. In tonight's episode, there's a character named the Soup Nazi—a really cranky guy who doesn't want to give customers his soup. I have trouble

44

hearing anything the people on the screen are saying because the laugh track is so loud. When the canned laughter
subsides for a moment, I decide to break the exciting news
about my day. "Mom, Dad, you won't believe who just
picked me up hitchhiking. Larry David!"

"Really? That's interesting. We love his stuff." Mom
points toward the glowing box and says, "Have you seen
this episode?"

Wait a minute—I just met the creator of the show they
love best, and this news registers a zero on the Parental
Richter Scale? But they are deeply into the Soup Nazi
plot, and can't be bothered with one of my mundane encounters. I guess their son's meeting and connecting with
Larry David isn't as interesting as watching one of his
shows.

Dad comments, "You've probably already seen this one."

"No. I, um, I never watch any television." (The clock
stops ticking.)

They both stare at me in horror, as if I've just told them
I'm a cannibal. "What? Wait. Never?"

Not to worry; I can bridge this gap. "Well now, which
one of these characters is Jerry?"

"Jerry is Jerry," Mom says.

"Okay. So Jason Alexander is Jason?"

"No," Dad chimes in. "Jason is George." My parents
burst into hysterics.

"How come you and the laugh track howl when the
guy with the strange haircut walks in?"

"Because Kramer is hilarious."

"But he didn't say anything yet."

"He's funny."

"But he didn't say anything; he just walked in."

Dad ignores my observations. "It's about life and other stuff . . ."

The soundtrack roars, and they laugh again. "You should sit down and watch this."

"No, thanks. Hey, I've got an idea. How about the three of us go down to the beach and watch the sunset? Maybe we could bring a blanket and a bottle of wine."

"Are you crazy?" Dad says in shock. "And miss *Seinfeld*?"

"But you watch these reruns every night."

"I've seen enough sunsets. Seen one, seen them all." And with that, he turns up the volume, and tunes me out.

CHAPTER 5

What Becomes of
the Brokenhearted

I retreat to my bedroom and pick up one of my favorite books, *The Prophet*. Every phrase in Kahlil Gibran's masterpiece feels divinely inspired. I open it to a random page and read, "The depth and connection of love is never truly known until the moment it is lost."

My phone rings, startling me from my reverie. Glancing at the caller ID, I see that it's her; the Miracle. Uh-oh . . . It's been a week since I fled Nashville, when she and I last spoke.

Ring Two . . .

Should I pick it up? I want to. I would so love to hear her soft voice . . .

Ring Three . . .

Maybe I shouldn't. What if this reopens all the old pain?

Ring Four . . .

Love or fear—which am I going to choose?

I take a deep breath, and then say, "Hello. I'm surprised you called."

There is a moment of silence. "Should I leave you alone?"

There is a longer silence on my part. "Ah, well . . . How's it going?"

"How are you doing?"

"Tell me about you. Anything new?"

"How's the island?"

"It's the Vineyard." Three beats. "The weather is beautiful."

"Nashville is so hot."

"It's cool here." Geez, we *never* talk about the weather. We share a couple of moments of awkward silence, and then exchange a few more superficial responses.

She sighs deeply. "I miss you."

I miss her as well. More than I could ever possibly say. But the words simply fail me. I'm not sure how long I remain mute as my mind wanders over miles of territory: The two of us smiling on a sunny beach in San Diego; a cozy candlelight dinner on an old wooden table; sharing an ice cream cone on a cool night; feeling betrayed; remembering my selfisÚess; periods of intense confusion; endless nights alone without sleep, lying in the void of darkness . . .

"Are you still there?"

"I'm sorry. My mind drifted off and ended up in a sad place."

"I'll let you go . . ."

"I thought you already had . . ."

"Was it me, or was it you?" Her voice breaks a little. "I'm sorry I called."

There is a click. And silence.

Funny; a part of me really wanted to connect, but as soon as I heard her voice, I shut down. Has there been a moment since my arrival when her ghost was not present on some level? No way. And yet . . .

What I wanted to say was: *How could we have done this to each other? We were given this beautiful, priceless love, and we pissed all over it. Why? Is there any way to put it all back together again? God, I miss you so much . . . I am so sorry. What happened to us?*

I sit there on the bed, my parents' television in the next room blaring the sounds of gunshots and wise guys exchanging witty repartee. When the numbness subsides, anger floods me, followed by a sense of bewilderment. How did I manage to lose her? Should I call her back and tell her to get on a plane? Where would we stay—at The Parental Asylum? Heavens, hasn't she suffered enough?

Maybe our separation is for the best. If there is any hope for me to heal, I will need more time and space. But my heart aches for her, and for us. Between my parents and the breakup, I feel like an unwelcomed, brokenhearted exile on the island of Elba.

"The depth and connection of love is never truly known until the moment it is lost," according to Gibran. Now I know, but somehow it feels too late.

For hours, I lie there in the darkness as my thoughts drift by. How has it all come to this? To end up without my girl, staying in my parents' home, sleeping on a mattress that was probably purchased during the Treaty of Versailles, adrift on the sea of life. What happened?

Unfortunately, the answers never come.

CHAPTER 6

Billionaires and Movie Stars

I wake up with what feels like a hangover. But instead of the usual headache, my whole being hurts. I guess even the shortest of interactions with the Miracle brings up boatloads of pain. How am I ever going to get over this? Lying around in this bed certainly isn't going to do it, so I leave the confines of The Parental Asylum and ride my bike down to Edgartown. It's a classic island morning of brisk sea breezes, low humidity, endless blue skies, swaying branches, strangers smiling and wishing one another well, and damp golden retrievers bouncing along with soggy tennis balls clenched between smiling fangs.

My spirits suddenly feel more buoyant, and in celebration of the day's perfection I take the long winding way past the harbor. The water looks even more blue than usual, as sailboats snatch the fervent wind and head for deep water. My destination is a humble one: a simple coffee shop.

One of the things I love about the Vineyard is its ability to equalize people socially. Here, the known and the unknown mingle freely. You may be a billionaire or even a movie star, but you still have to wait in line for your cappuccino at Espresso Love. The inside of the café is about the size of a large walk-in closet, but it boasts a covered porch and a small garden where large dogs and vagrants like me are welcome. The shop is run efficiently by a swarm of girls who manage to keep everyone happy and highly caffeinated.

Today finds me on the porch with fellow Espresso regular Billionaire Bob. He and I met at this very place six summers ago, and have grown closer over a series of coffees and egg sandwiches. We spend a cheerful thirty minutes covering the sports scene and catching up on island news. Though extremely wealthy, he's one of the least pretentious men I have ever met. He's also one of the smartest, and with his thick glasses and mad-scientist hairdo he really looks the part.

"How's your summer going so far?" Bob asks in his thick Boston-Irish accent.

"Pretty good, other than a little heartbreak."

"So there was a girl . . ."

"A lovely girl . . ."

"There's always a girl." He folds and puts down his newspaper. "Can it be fixed?"

"I'm not sure."

"Romantic relationships are the toughest thing in the world. They're also the most rewarding."

"I need to find some clarity. I haven't felt this confused since I saw the movie *Memento*."

He smiles. "I'm sure you'll be okay. Are you working on anything right now?"

"I'm between bad ideas." He flashes another smile. "Seriously, I feel like I'm in a place between. Almost like when the trapeze artist releases one bar while floating toward another. There is that moment of perfect stillness between the two, where there is neither this nor that; a kind of suspension. It certainly feels like a moment of faith."

I stop; there is silence for a few seconds. To fill the space, I move the focus from myself and ask, "What would you say drives you?"

He considers this for a few moments, takes a long, slow sip of his coffee, and looks out over the courtyard. "I'll tell you the dirty little secret of ambition: a deep sense of inadequacy. Of wanting to prove something and never feeling like you're enough."

Considering his vast success, this catches me off-guard, "You feel that way?"

He nods. "I'd like to think I've gotten better over the years, but sometimes I have to wonder."

There is a moment of deep intimacy between us, and then suddenly a sense of awkwardness transpires. Did I cross some imaginary line here?

Bob glances at his watch. "Good Lord, look at the time. I'd better run. I have a million calls to make."

I reach out my hand to him. "Thanks for being so honest." He shakes my hand and then with a sly smile says, "Don't tell anyone my secrets."

"You're safe."

As he wanders toward his bike, he peers back over the fence. "Hey, I'm sorry about the girl."

I nod, force a smile, and give him a halfhearted wave.

Did we simply get too close, or did I just experience The Billionaire Lean-back?

I've noticed that many wealthy people suffer from this affliction. My Lean-back Theory goes something like this: Proximity might lead to intimacy, intimacy might lead to trust, and trust might lead to asking for money. So if you can avoid proximity, intimacy, and trust, you can definitely avoid being hit up for cash.

Here's how it works: Someone approaches a wealthy or famous person with the secret intent of getting them to part with some of their vast wealth. It could be a business venture to invest in, a medical need, some harebrained scheme, or a plain old-fashioned handout. But the bottom line is: Show me the money! After being approached countless times by family, friends, or strangers looking for a piece of their gigantic nest eggs and connections, the individual begins instinctively to lean back. At times this is done literally in terms of body language, but more often it is a pulling back of interpersonal connection. Who can they trust? After a while, every encounter becomes a potential awkward request for something. So, unless the person they run into is also wealthy, or has a long history of being in the billionaire's proximity without seeking a handout, they are treated with trepidation. Perhaps Bob thought I was going to ask for some kind of help when I said I was in between things, despite the fact that I've never hit him up for anything before. Judging by the way he suddenly fled, I felt as if something had been triggered.

It struck me that most of us think we'd like to be wealthy, powerful, and famous, yet these are the very things that isolate celebrities and the super-rich from others, and from a true sense of self.

I get back on my bike and ride up the Edgartown–West Tisbury Road. The meandering path takes me to the Morning Glory farm stand. Started in 1975, it encompasses fifty acres of vegetables and fruits, which are in evidence in its amazing salad bar. Feeling a little hungry, I decide to pull into the dirt parking lot.

A few old biodegradable hands and a lot of young, eager summer kids populate the sprawling farm. All seem to share an aversion to soap and water; perhaps they envision bathing, grooming, and shaving as the first step toward being co-opted by the corporate world. Mainstream hygiene aside, the ragtag crew always appears to be joyful and enthusiastic.

The salad bar is a glorious organic hodgepodge of color, aroma, and taste. The offerings have come straight out of the ground and into my bowl. I grab one of their culinary creations and take my tomatoes, cucumbers, peppers, and fresh lettuce to an old wooden bench that sits in the shade of a giant oak.

Staring at the greens in front of me, I am struck by their perfection. These things grow freely in dirt, yet they provide the energy I need to ride a bike, swim, hitch a ride, wrangle with my parents. I look around at the various plants, trees, flowers, weeds, and whatnot bursting from every corner of the farm stand. Picking up a perfect piece of sweet corn and admiring its bright yellow kernels, I take a bite and sigh.

A tiny brown bird lands on the picnic table only two feet from my hand. I look at this beautiful little thing and say, "Well, hello." My new guest cocks his head and considers me for a few moments, and then spontaneously bursts into song. He pauses for a second—overly dramatically, I think—and then continues with the second movement of his Sparrow Symphony in E-flat.

Where in the heck did this creature come from?

So . . . we know that the earth was covered in molten lava for a few billion years. Then it cooled off. Then it rained for millions more years. The oceans withdrew. Eons go by, and then one day the place is teeming. All kinds of life-forms emerge from the primordial soup: giraffes, whales, vegans, this little brown bird, Billionaire Bob, the golden mutt sniffling the basket of tomatoes over there, and me; we all come from the same source—stardust. The concept is absolutely mind blowing.

The little brown guy must like my stream of thought, because he breaks into another one of his greatest hits. I look at the world around me, and I feel my rough edges become a little smoother; everything seems strikingly vivid, more alive.

My feathered friend is giving me an intense look. I take a long, deep breath and experience an overwhelming sensation of oneness—with the bird, the fields of corn, the endless sky, the whole shebang. I sense that in some strange way, the bird returns the feeling.

Then again, perhaps I'm out of my mind, and he simply wants a piece of my crouton.

CHAPTER 7

Jewish Sailing

Energized by my Morning Glory Farm moments, I climb back on my bike and head down the tree-lined path. Soon my wheels cross the West Tisbury border (no passport required). Stopping on a small bridge, I come upon a regal swan silently cruising the pond. She passes a few feet from me, considers me briefly, and then gracefully glides forward, all of her locomotive efforts elegantly hidden from the naked eye. The reeds blow and the water lilies stir as I pause to take in the stillness, the presence, and the peace.

My next destination is Alley's General Store. This funky little hole-in-the-wall was founded about 150 years ago, which also happens to be the last time it was cleaned. Okay, I'm exaggerating; it's actually charming. Alley's is a convenient stop for any wayfarer headed up-island, which makes it a fertile spot for hitchhiking. And there's a real voodoo to the place. No matter how random my request might be, every time I walk in, I find exactly what I desire.

"Do you happen to have organic, blueberry, raccoon's-milk nonfat ice cream with raisins?"

"Yes, it's right across from the nuclear fusion set."

Today, though, I keep it simple with a cup of coffee. My legs are feeling a little sore, so I decide to ditch my wheels. I walk out and across the parking lot, lean my bike against a tree, and stick out my thumb to summon the infinite possibilities of the moment.

My first ride looks as if it drove straight out of *The Great Gatsby:* a candy-red, vintage Mercedes convertible with beige leather seats. The driver, Mike, is handsome with thick, black curly hair and a welcoming smile.

"Hop in, hitchhiker."

"Thanks, partner." The car pulls out of the lot. Abiding by The Official MVY Hitchhiker's Manifesto, I ask, "Are you on vacation?"

"No, I unintentionally ended up with the whole summer off." I look at him curiously, and he continues. "I was recently downsized."

"I'm sorry."

"Don't be. It was difficult at first, but probably for the best." Mike reaches up to adjust the rearview mirror. "I was burned out on the whole Wall Street charade and ready for a change. The job was sucking the life out of me. The merger just hurried me out the door."

"So, now what?"

"To tell you the truth, I have no idea. My being here all season is part of the process of discovering what's next."

"Any luck?"

"None. I have no earthly idea what the future holds for me."

I extend my hand. "Join the club." We shake as I add, "I guess we've become high-end Vineyard vagrants."

"That's a nice way to look at it. How long are you here?"

"A couple of weeks. Unless my dad runs me off early."

"Back at home, are you?"

Man, do I really want to admit to another man around my age that I have completely failed at the game of life and did not pass Go or collect two hundred dollars? Hell, why not. "And you thought being fired was depressing. Yes, I am back at home."

"What about staying at the campground?"

"I would, but I look awful in a wife-beater."

Mike laughs. "Hey, brother, this recent economic meltdown has a lot of people moving in with someone, and it's got me questioning my old values. For years, I worked my ass off and made a lot of money. But in the end, it left me empty. At this stage in my life, I feel like I'm reevaluating everything."

Although we are strangers, our conversation has become surprisingly personal. Wall Street Mike is very open and honest about his feelings, finances, and fears. I realize that maybe being two dudes around the same age, on the same island, at the same time—trying to figure out the chessboard of our lives in a tricky time of transition—provides an instantaneous bond. It seems as if Mike has been waiting a long time to share his feelings—if only someone would be kind enough to ask. Maybe we're all like that: just waiting for a chance to reveal ourselves.

"Speaking of money, how are you dealing with being out of work? Are you sleeping okay?" I ask.

Mike smiles. "Actually I've been sleeping very deeply ever since I got here."

"It's amazing how the Vineyard does that."

I know that the rules of society clearly state that we should all mind our own business and keep the topics on a highly superficial level. "Howareyou?" "Fineandyou?" Preferably these lines are said while not missing a beat, taking a breath, or, most important, making any kind of authentic connection. But maybe with a genuine desire to bond, we can break through the inauthentic ice. I don't mind being the catalyst for intimacy; in fact, I like it. Which is why I love to hitchhike. Each encounter carries the potential for a deeper connection, if only for the fifteen-minute duration of the ride. Or as Mark Twain so eloquently said, "Nothing so liberalizes a man and expands the kindly instincts that nature put in him as travel and contact with many kinds of people."

It's as if each person carries innate wisdom buried deep within. These truths may emerge when one asks the right question, or, more important, when one allows enough space between the answers.

The vintage ride winds along the picturesque South Road, past rolling fields, rambling stone walls, and occasional glimpses of the mighty Atlantic Ocean.

Mike glances over at me. "I'll bet you meet some interesting people hitchhiking."

"You have no idea." I wonder if I should tell him about my recent ride, then decide to go ahead. "Just yesterday I was picked up by Larry David."

"The *Seinfeld* guy?"

"Yes."

"Man, I love his stuff. Especially *Curb Your Enthusiasm*."

"He was very interesting."

"Was he a real curmudgeon, like his character on the show?"

I duck the question about watching his show, but add, "Actually I found him to be a wonderful person."

"Larry David?"

I laugh. "We covered a lot of ground, and not because he took me all the way up to Aquinnah. He shared some pretty interesting deep thoughts with me."

"Are we talking about the same Larry David?"

I nod. "Believe me, I was pretty surprised. Hell, I still am. It was kind of surreal. But less than twenty-four hours ago, the two of us were driving along this very road."

Mike shakes his head for a moment or two, trying to wrap his mind around all this. "Did you see the *Curb* episode about hitchhiking?"

"No, I never have." This comment makes me wonder if this would be the episode to lose my *Curb* virginity on. "What happens?"

"It's hysterical. He picks up this prostitute on his way to a Dodgers game so he can avoid traffic and use the HOV lane. Unfortunately, once he's at the stadium, he runs into some people he knows, and it becomes a typical LD mess."

"That is wild. So it sounds like his life is imitating his art."

"Don't tell me you're a prostitute." Mike cocks his eyebrow.

"Is there a market for guys like me?" I put my hands on my hips and strike a seductive pose.

He laughs. "Probably not, but hey, you never know. Do you like *Seinfeld*?"

"I've never seen it."

"You're kidding, right?"

"Apparently I am a minority of one."

Mike shakes his head in disbelief. "Where have you been the last ten years?"

"All over the place, but not in front of a television set."

"I hope you didn't tell Larry that little fact."

"Believe it or not, it came up."

"What did he say?"

"He threatened to throw me out of the car. I have the distinction of being Larry's first hitchhiker. And based on the experience, I'll probably be his last. Actually we ended up making a deal. I have until the end of the summer to watch at least one of his programs."

"Check out *Curb;* you'll love it. You know what's really crazy? Larry lives a couple of miles up the road from me in this tiny town of Chilmark, and I have never once seen him."

"Not once?"

"Never!"

"That's the beauty of this place. It's easy to get lost here if you want to. Most of the residents don't harass their famous neighbors, who definitely don't want to stand out. It's sort of an unwritten island code."

As we approach Beetlebung Corner, I ask, "Can you drop me in front of the Chilmark Store?"

Mike pulls over and extends his hand. "It was great meeting you. I hope our paths cross again."

"Me too."

"Larry David, huh? Really?"

"On this very road."

Mike shakes his head. I get out of the Mercedes and close the door. "Thanks for the ride. I hope you figure things out."

"I hope I see you again. Hey, good luck with your dad." And he's off.

Wandering up the weathered wooden steps of the store, I'm immediately reminded of why I love this place: the classic New England porch with its randomly scattered rocking chairs, people from all walks of life immersed in conversation, kids running around with Popsicle-stained faces, and the smell of the island's best pizza wafting through the salty sea air.

I grab my first slice of the season and take a front-row seat with an unobstructed view of the festivities. Ah, the joy of the very first bite. The pizza is warm, crisp, and perfectly seasoned. The pepperoni has a little kick to it, and the basil must have come from a local garden. My mouth is watering from the aroma alone.

Soon I'm chatting with one of the local celebrities, Harold Ramis, who has had enormous success in the film business: acting (*Ghostbusters*), directing (*Groundhog Day, Caddyshack, Analyze This*), and writing (*Animal House, Ghostbusters* along with Dan Aykroyd). Harold is a great storyteller, and today is no exception. He describes the follies surrounding the promotion of his latest film, and I give him my rapt attention.

Alan Dershowitz arrives and sits across from us. A Harvard Law professor and sometimes controversial figure, Alan has defended many high-profile clients, like O. J. Simpson (still out there hunting for the "real killers") and the notorious Claus Von Bülow. The film *Reversal of Fortune* was based on Alan's book about that case. But today, Alan is just another guy in an old shirt on his way to the beach.

In the midst of this enjoyable chaos, a woman around my age asks, "Do you mind if I sit here?" I nod to welcome her, and she plops down next to me with her own slice. "I'm Nancy." We shake hands and start raving about the pizza.

"Where are you from?" I ask.

"Beverly Hills, though I hate to tell people. I'm not sure I fit in there."

I can see why. She exudes none of the pretension (or Botox) usually associated with that zip code. She seems more natural, like someone from Vermont who raises autistic goats on an organic farm.

"Why do you feel like you don't fit in out there?"

"There are a lot of reasons. The pace, it's so materialistic, and I hate all the traffic." She pauses and looks around. "I really like it here."

"Me too."

She thinks for a minute. "I guess the hardest part of being there has been trying to raise my three kids consciously, and especially watching my teenage boy struggle. He's a great kid, but we've had a lot of ups and downs with him. Los Angeles is a tough place to be a teenager."

"I find it a tough place to be a biped."

"You're right." She smiles. "It's been a stressful couple of years, but hopefully we've turned a corner. I'm sorry; I didn't mean to dump all this on you."

"Don't apologize for being authentic; I'm flattered. I can't imagine what it feels like to raise a child and then surrender that precious being to society. I've never had the courage to have a kid."

"Maybe someday you will."

"Maybe."

"Are you married?"

"No, and my long-term relationship just went up in flames. Perhaps I should find a bride through the Internet."

"Do you speak any Russian?"

"That mail-order bride thing scares me. You send for the woman, and then six months later 'Uncle Boris' moves in with you."

She laughs.

"I've decided to give it six more months, and if I still haven't met anyone, I'm going to Lourdes."

"I think there's a certain amount of luck involved in meeting someone you can really connect with. Then you have to have the commitment, desire, and resilience to make it work. It's hard enough for two people to make it, but then when you add children to the mix, everything gets a lot more complex."

"All of that sounds intimidating."

She chuckles. "Don't be discouraged. It's a process; you adapt as you go. Oh, there's my husband." She waves him over.

A tiny guy with perfectly coiffed silver hair and matching beard comes flying over and shakes my hand. He seems a tad high-strung; he doesn't actually look at me because he's too busy scanning the porch. After a moment, he steps away to schmooze with a far more important life-form.

Nancy shares a secret. "He wouldn't want me to tell you this because he's so private, but he's a very successful power broker in Hollywood and New York."

"What does he do?"

"He raises money for films and other projects."

"Does he enjoy it?"

She looks down at her lap. "You'd have to ask him."

Watching him flutter around the porch from fiefdom to fiefdom, I realize that he could pass for some kind of highly caffeinated prehistoric bird—a species that survived by avoiding much deadlier predators who evolved over time into the people now running large corporations.

The Hollywood Birdman returns and, after a few minutes of pleasant give-and-take, surprises me with "Would you like to join us for a little Jewish sailing?"

"A little what?"

"Jewish sailing. Come on, we'll have fun." Having never experienced Jewish sailing, I am intrigued and say yes.

We get into their car, me sitting in back, and drive down to the dock. We climb into his high-tech motorboat, and he guns it. The sun dances off the frothing wake as we spin around the gorgeous confines of Menemsha Pond. It's a picture-perfect day, the scenery is stunning, and there's a chill in the air. Ever since I was a kid, I have loved being on the water.

The captain inquires, "Well, what do you think? Peaceful, yes?"

I nod. "It's wonderful, and reminds me of my first days in a boat a long time ago . . ."

It is a cloudless Sunday morning. In our small rented rowboat, we leave civilization and venture deep into the backwaters of the Florida Everglades in search of fish. With his ever-present two-dollar transistor radio in hand, Dad soaks up the scenery. I listen to the tinny sound of the Carpenters' tune "Top of the World," perfectly capturing the moment in song. My dad reminds me that this is a far cry from the Brooklyn tenement he grew up in.

My friend Jeff and I dutifully do the oar work. It's demanding, but, inspired by the beauty of our surroundings, the ten-year-old crew is not complaining. The alligators eye us warily from the shore. On second thought, it's we who are leery of them.

We come out here a lot, and often we allow the current to take us where it wishes. We watch cranes stalk fish, and otters play with the abandon of children. Though we rarely ever catch anything, nothing takes away from our reverence for this aquatic cathedral.

Those early years with Dad were golden. Even though he was working hard to support his young family, he always had time for me and my younger brother, Chris. He coached every team, took us to the beach, taught us to throw—the guy was amazing.

Dad was also warm and affectionate when I was a kid. He would kiss me on the forehead in public and tell me he loved me. He was encouraging, funny, and engaging. He was tall, dark, and handsome, with a natural charisma that attracted all types of people. He regaled us with exotic stories of growing up in Brooklyn, and of serving during World War Two in China, India, and the jungles of Burma. No one knew more about films, music, culture, or politics. I simply worshiped the guy.

But when I got into my teenage years, Dad fell into a deep funk and began to disengage. Thirty years later, I feel as if I'm still waiting for him to emerge, snap out of it, and start smiling again. To kiss me once again on the forehead and tell me how much he loves me. But maybe this desire is hopeless.

Birdman looks at me, "Are you okay?"

"Just caught me in a daydream."

He raises his arms and says, "Jewish sailing!"

Since we never perform any religious rituals during the expedition, I fail to discover the difference between Jewish and, say, Hindu sailing. Maybe it's because we got into the boat, simply turned a key, leisurely went back and forth, never left the pond, had something sweet to eat, and didn't break a sweat; mostly we just kibitzed.

As we pull into the dock and grab our stuff, I deliver the famous *Godfather* line, "Leave the gun; take the cannoli." Nancy points to her husband and says, "That's the one he always uses!" This must be a secret bonding code, because Birdman surprises me again with "Would you like to come back and see our place?"

Nancy looks at me suddenly, and her face takes on an interesting expression while I consider the invite. She catches my eye and ever-so-subtly nods, letting me know that it's fine for me to say yes.

At Nancy's prompt, I go with the flow. "Sure. That would be great."

Birdman seems pleased. As he walks down the street to get the Jeep, Nancy lets me in on another secret. "I'm kind of shocked. My husband is one of the most private people you'll ever meet. He never invites strangers to go boating, and even our friends rarely come to our home."

"It must be the new cologne."

She laughs. "I'm telling you, this is very out of character. So many people want something from him, and his job is so socially demanding that he needs his solitary time here on the Vineyard to rejuvenate."

"That makes sense."

"I'm just amazed that he has opened up to you."

"Well, I'll wait until we get back to the house to pitch my film idea and ask for money."

She laughs and shakes her head. "You'd be surprised what people ask him for."

Within minutes, we're making our way down a winding driveway. We come upon a low-key compound of several small buildings that overlooks one of the prettiest beaches I have ever seen. The views are breathtaking; from here, you can see all the way up the whole north shore, straight to the multicolored cliffs of Aquinnah. It looks as if there was a recent mudslide that took out a vast portion of the property. The sea seems to be advancing on the land's turf; the cliffs appear diminished from the water's onslaught. A small flock of seagulls float on invisible breezes in front of us.

I point to the group of hovering white angels. "I wish I could do that."

Birdman considers this for a moment and says, "Don't

get too ethereal on me, kid, or I'll make you fly back to your bike."

Breathing in the sea air, I take stock of the view. With the humidity low, the fog has decided to take the night off. The waves crash on the shore, far below our lofty perch. It's paradise.

Birdman beckons to me. "Hey, tumbleweed, come on in for a drink."

While we're relaxing on the back deck, Nancy says, "Remember, you have a golf date tomorrow with Larry."

My radar goes off. Going for broke, I ask, "Is that Larry David, by chance?"

"Yes," Birdman replies suspiciously. "How did you know?"

"He picked me up hitchhiking yesterday."

"No he didn't."

"I'm serious; he did."

"But Larry never picks up hitchhikers!"

"He did. I swear."

"Don't lie to me."

"Call him and ask him."

He ponders this, sizes me up, then texts Larry the cryptic message. *I'm sitting in my living room with Nancy and the hitchhiker . . .*

"He picked you up?"

"He was very gracious."

"Are you sure it was Larry?"

This makes me laugh. "Hey, I'd better get back to my bike before dark. I still have a long ride back to Edgartown."

"Nice to meet you, kid. Come back and see us again sometime."

This makes Nancy smile. "Come on, I'll give you a lift."

She gives me a quick ride back to Alley's for my bike, and a few minutes later I'm pedaling toward home. About halfway there, I come to a fork in the road. I can go to my parents' place for dinner, or head into Edgartown, where the cell signal is strong enough to return a few phone calls. Though hungry, I choose the latter. I have no idea at the time, but this simple decision will set the tone for my entire summer.

CHAPTER 8

The Larry Phenomenon

I arrive in Edgartown during the magic hour: that time of the day when the light is soft and the hues are warm. This village looks like something Walt Disney would have created and called "New England Town."

Coming down Main Street feels like riding into a postcard: immaculate houses repainted annually in white; manicured gardens with pristine picket fences; the police directing traffic on narrow one-way streets; small shops lining the lanes; and sitting stoically at the top of Main in all her colonial splendor, the historic Whaling Church. This stately landmark, an example of Greek Revival architecture, was built in 1843 by local whaling captains, who used wood from their retired ships.

Turning left down Water Street, I pass hundred-year-old captains' houses, with their widow's walks and roses in full bloom. I can smell the honeysuckle blossoms as I ride by quaint cottages with welcoming front porches. The sun floods the harbor with a palette of pastels, showering streaks of light upon me and its gently bobbing vessels. I stop at the Edgartown Wharf to return my calls, but for some strange reason I fail to get a signal.

On the move again, I run into Mr. Flakey. In the past, we have shared an annual exercise in futility. It takes a few minutes, but then we start our familiar dance steps and fall back into what I have christened . . .

MR. FLAKEY'S TANGO

Stage One: We bump into each other, talk for a while, and he tells me to call him to set up a time for us to have lunch.

> My interpretation: Call me for lunch. = Call me for lunch.

> Actual meaning: Call me for lunch. = Don't really call, but it's good to see you.

Stage Two: I call and leave a message; he never calls back.

Stage Three: We run into each other again, he says he never got the message, claims to have lost my number, really wants to get together, asks me to call him again to set a time for us to definitely have lunch. I try to say maybe another time, but he is insistent that we make a date.

My interpretation: Really wants to get together = Really wants to get together.

Actual meaning: Really wants to get together = Damn, not him again.

Stage Four: I call and leave another message; again he doesn't call back. We engage in more awkward encounters. It gets to the point where he sees me coming and avoids me; I see him coming and avoid him.

Stage Five: Return to island and begin Stage One again . . .

This summer we are right on schedule when, after a few minutes of small talk, Mr. Flakey resumes our dance. I try to politely decline, but as in all the times before, he presses his number into my hand and insists I call him to make a lunch date. I stow the piece of paper in my pocket, realizing that some people are just limited in their ability to see things through. If we happen to run into each other, he can make the most of the momentary connection. But to actually plan something is an entirely different animal.

I say good-bye to Mr. Flakey and start looking for a signal strong enough to converse cellularly. I want to call the Miracle back and see if we can do a better job of connecting. With my phone in front of me like a divining rod, I find a bench overlooking the harbor and begin to make my call. I'm dialing when I see someone approaching from the corner of my eye.

"Excuse me, do you happen to know where the Atlantic restaurant . . . Oh my God."

I hang up the phone. "Larry?"

Larry asks, "Are you a ghost or something?"

"Uh, no, I'm not a ghost! But . . ."

"Then how did . . ."

"Did you get the text about me being on Birdman's deck?"

"Yes. It sort of freaked me out. Wait a minute; are you on your bike?"

"Yes."

"So you rode about twenty miles?"

"I did. Nancy dropped me at Alley's Store, where I'd left my bike."

"How did you get down here so fast?"

I consider this for a moment, then reply, "I pedaled a lot?"

"So you were with them at their house?"

"Well, first we went Jewish sailing."

"What the hell is that?"

"I'm still not sure."

"How did you end up back at his house?"

"He invited me."

"Did you know them from before?"

"No, we met a couple of hours ago."

"And they took you Jewish . . . What the hell did you call it?"

"Jewish sailing . . ."

"Right . . . and then back to their house?"

"Yes . . ."

"A total stranger they just met . . ."

"I guess they were feeling pretty friendly . . ."

"How did I come up?"

"Nancy mentioned something about his golf date with Larry . . ."

"And you knew it was me."

"Is there another Larry on the island?"

He chuckles. "But how did you know it was me?"

"I just had a feeling . . ."

He nods . . . "But how did you meet them?"

"We met over pizza and then went Jewish sailing."

"What the hell is that again?"

"I told you, I don't know . . ."

Larry takes a few moments to ponder this and uses his hands to point between imaginary places, maybe in an effort to figure out the logistics of all this. "And you were in their living room when he texted me?"

"Yes. He didn't believe you picked me up."

"Why did you come to Edgartown?"

"I came here to make some calls . . ."

"And I got lost looking for that restaurant . . ."

"What are the odds of something like this happening?"

Larry thinks for a moment. "The timing . . . it's almost impossible." He looks intensely at me, at the bike, his phone . . . then at me again . . . "It's crazy!"

He starts to walk away, then turns back. "Wait a minute—where the hell is the restaurant?"

I point over his shoulder. "It's that place there on the water."

"Thanks. I'd better go; I'm late." He takes a few steps

and then turns around. He raises his hand as if to make a point, and then shakes his head. "Something's going on here."

"I agree. Should we go to lunch and figure it out?"

"No."

I laugh.

Then he adds, "But I'm going to think about it and see if I can make some sense of it."

"Please let me know if you do." He smiles and waves, and off he goes.

I text Birdman and tell him what has just happened. His response is oddly philosophical, given his previous no-nonsense manner. "You seem to be in a very strong place of attraction right now. Be extremely conscious of what you choose to create."

His comment reminds me of *Star Wars,* when Obi-Wan Kenobi says, "Use the Force, Luke." Maybe Birdman has a deep, poetic side that only comes out in rare moments.

In the wake of Larry's departure, I consider the timing required for this odd coincidence to have occurred. Then I ponder the deeper implications of chance and luck in our lives. Change a moment here or a moment there, and every single thing in someone's life can turn out completely different. It's incredible how our future can shift with the simplest of random choices. If I hadn't accepted my friend's invitation to spend Christmas in Del Mar—which I almost didn't—I never would have met the Miracle and lived with her for two years. If I hadn't gotten a job at that particular gas station in Nashville and met the executive, I probably wouldn't have gotten into the music business. But if everything hangs in such a delicate balance, how can we feel as if we have any influence over our own destinies?

I'm reminded of the words of Albert Einstein: "Everything is determined . . . by forces over which we have no control. It is determined for the insect, as well as for the star. Human beings, vegetables, or cosmic dust, we all dance to a mysterious tune, intoned in the distance by an invisible piper."

I smile, put my headphones back on, and press play. The Beatles begin singing "All You Need Is Love."

The harbor becomes even more dazzling, as a vast panoply of boats finds its way back from the darkening horizon. A sleek sailboat embossed with the moniker BELIEVE pulls directly in front of me. I consider this for a moment or two. Did I believe that the Miracle and I could work through our problems if we gave it another try? I try dialing again, but the call won't go through.

CHAPTER 9

Island Life

It is the Fourth of July and I wake up to my mother's beaming smile. The early morning, with its whispers of coastal fog lingering throughout the woods, is our special time together before Dad wakes up and the 'rents merge into a single entity dedicated to solving the world's crossword puzzles. Once a fierce emotional bulldozer of hectoring advice, Mom has mellowed and become more childlike.

"Good morning," she says. We hug and kiss. Her skin feels moist, and the fragrance of her favorite Avon product lingers on my cheek. "Would you like an omelet?"

"I can fix it myself, Mom."

"I'll make it for you." My mother likes to be the boss of her domestic domain. She picks up a small notepad and pen. "There's so much to do; I should make a list. Are you hungry? Can I make you an omelet for breakfast?"

"Yes, that sounds great."

Over the past year, she has begun shedding her short-term memory. Yet in a twist of karmic brilliance, the more she forgets, the more laid-back and nurturing she becomes.

I follow her into the kitchen. Max comes up and nudges my mother's leg. She bends down to pet his black-and-gold fur and says, "Oh look, he's letting me know he wants his breakfast."

Knowing she always feeds him the minute she gets up, I say, "Mom, I think you already fed the little beggar." Suspecting I may be on to his food con, Max gives me a guilty sideways glance. At some point, he must have figured out that Mom is like a broken ATM, capable of yielding an unending stream of kibble, and has decided to milk this for all it's worth.

Mom bends down with his second of potentially innumerable breakfasts. "Here's your food, little fella." Max waddles over to his grub, looks up at me as if to say, *Don't be a snitch,* and chows down. Since we're fellow inmates, I remain silent.

I watch my mother as she stands there beaming at her dog, noting her serene features. To me, she is still beautiful. "You look terrific, Mom."

Pleased, she chuckles to herself. "Would you like some breakfast?"

I smile. "That would be great. Are there any of those free-range eggs that I bought left over?"

She frowns slightly, and I drop it. Although my mother has mellowed quite a bit, you still need to be careful where you step.

Maternal Conversational Land Mines
to Avoid at Any Cost

- The United States of America (Still the greatest country in the world!)

- The mold growing in her house (What the hell can I do about it?)

- Non-organic food (I've lived eighty years eating this poison.)

- Dad (Don't criticize your father!)

- Max's getting fat (He's the perfect size for his breed!)

Facts be damned; she knows what she knows, and she is always right. Her certainty is based on Einstein's Theory of Obscurity: Longevity = Knowledge[6]. I'm curious about the phenomenon of Mom's gaining knowledge through linear time osmosis, as opposed to more traditional methods such as research or personal experience. When asked about this, she offers no insights. Instead, she dismisses my inquiries with a shake of her head. "I'm not going to get into it," she declares.

As her dementia increases, I feel as if my mother, although still present physically, is sadly missing. Perhaps there is a tiny hole somewhere in her being, and her personality is gradually leaking out into the ether. Yes, she can still talk without a break for more than an hour, but she might repeat the same statement a dozen times. Since everything we share is lost, there is no context to hold anything in perspective. A story, an anecdote, an observation, an opinion, a feeling; it's all as fleeting as the ticking from the old Swiss clock laboring away on the cluttered wall.

Over the past couple of winters when I've visited them in Florida, I have seen this memory thief slowly creep into the chambers of her mind and steal her capacity for recall. All of it—no matter how important, or how trivial—evaporates before my eyes, into the abyss.

Whenever I bring up the possibility of her trying one of the new and promising medications to slow her deterioration, my father instantly kills the idea with no allowance for debate. This is surprising because for years, my parents have been going to a phalanx of doctors for anything short of a hangnail. They take a variety of medications to regulate their sedentary forms, and completely believe that if someone is wearing a white coat with a stethoscope, he or she has the unerring capacity to prescribe away their troubles.

But for some reason, Dad refuses to bring up Mom's rapid memory loss to their primary physician, or to let Mom be tested for it.

My pervading conspiracy theory is he actually likes the defanged version of Momzilla better than the old Irish pit bull. The "Old Mom" had the audacity to desire annoying things he didn't particularly care for—such as:

1) Spending money

2) Leaving the house

3) Fixing anything that was broken

4) Interacting with other life-forms

5) Spending money

The two of them passed the majority of my life waging war with each other over the vast battleground of their differences. Mom used traditional combat tecÚiques like the full-frontal attack (vitriolic, emasculating verbal assaults), while Dad was a guerrilla fighter (canceling a much-anticipated vacation or trip at the very last second by feigning illness).

So conspiracy buffs like me suspect that this new benign, distracted, unmotivated, confused, pliable, kinder Mom is more to Sneaky Dad's liking.

This morning Mom spontaneously says, "I would like to go to Morning Glory today and buy some plants."

"Hey, come here and look at the feeder," Sneaky Dad says, completely ignoring her request. "There's a cute little bird out here."

Mom gets up and looks out the window. "What was I saying? Oh yes, I'd like to get some plants today and maybe do a little gardening."

"What time does that nature show you love come on?"

"I'm not sure . . ."

"Would you like some more coffee?"

"No, thank you. What was I saying?"

"You were talking about your nature show."

"I was? Oh, what time does it come on?"

Of course the last thing Dad wants is a witness to his shenanigans, so that's another reason on the ever-mounting list of "Why I'm Not Welcome." If I do interject with an offer to take Mom to any of her desired destinations, Dad will give me a withering glance or threaten me with immediate eviction.

In the past, I have foolishly tried to play relationship referee to their fifty-year dysfunction. The results at best were disastrous.

While many people become bitter with age (i.e., Dad), Mom is being transformed from a disenchanted cynic into someone who is just happy to be here. So in the polarity of my parents' universe, Mom is the positive Yin to Dad's cranky Yang.

As Mom's social self crumbles away, something infinitely more luminous is emerging. This radiance is what I see when I gaze into her eyes. Again, I say, "Mom, you really do look great."

"Really?" She glances at herself in the mirror and strokes her hair, now streaked with gray. "Well, I'm a few inches shorter than my modeling days back in New York." In her heyday, Mom was one of the top runway models in the city, and helped support her family with the money she earned strolling the catwalk. She looks in the mirror again. "But I guess I'm not bad for my age."

"Mom, you look absolutely radiant. I think I'm going to ride the bike down to Edgartown and enjoy some of the festivities."

The Fourth of July in Edgartown is a classic piece of Americana. On the big day, the town decks itself out in flags and banners, and there is a palpable festivity in the air. People flood the town from all over the island. This is as crowded as you will ever see the place, yet no one is cranky. In fact, the opposite is unfolding: laughter, smiles, polite exchanges, and high-fives.

The holiday highlight is certainly the old-time parade.

Coming straight out of a time machine, it is replete with vintage fire engines, classic cars, bagpipes, marching bands, drummers, clubs, and local folks sitting in the back of well-worn pickup trucks. Many of the homemade floats carry enthusiastic people tossing candy to the throngs of young children who eagerly line the streets, their innocent faces filled with joy and wonder at the passing procession. Mothers carrying babies, fathers with infants on their shoulders, old folks in plastic beach chairs, cool young guys with skateboards—we are all here.

For me, the whole thing is a beautiful snapshot of small-town America, harking back to a simpler time. Of the enduring power of community and the uncomplicated love for one's country. As the tiny makeshift band rips into a highly spirited version of JoÚ Philip Sousa's "Stars and Stripes Forever," I feel the goose bumps rise across my body and a lump fills my throat.

A ragged band of veterans of our many wars marches by, and several of us spontaneously yell out, "Thank you!" The vets smile and acknowledge our gratitude for their sacrifice and service.

When the parade is finished, the mob heads down to the harbor for the traditional fireworks display. The crowd responds to the explosions with the customary "Oooo—ahhhh . . ." and applause. I'm lying on the beach a few yards from the Edgartown Lighthouse, soaking it all in. My stomach is filled with a couple of hot dogs whose purchase benefited some worthy cause, and a couple of scoops of Oreo cookie ice cream.

For the moment, life seems good.

A couple of days later, the television is blaring around-the-clock coverage of Michael Jackson's death. (This is the top story on the planet?) Catching a few minutes of his funeral on the tube, being held at the sold-out Staples Center, I'm struck by the way in which the service resembles a musical variety show with a twist: There is a large gold casket on stage. In between performances from people who have never even met the king of pop, and maudlin tributes by celebrities, the advertisers try to sell me stuff I don't really need. I stop and wonder if at some point I went through one of those strange dimensional portals and ended up in a parallel universe where what passes for reality is something very foreign to me.

Deciding to leave my parents to MJ's tribute, I get on my bike for the ten-mile ride up to Alley's. The day is unusually hot and humid, rare for the Vineyard, so my shirt is soaked by the time I reach my destination.

Popping into the store, I head straight for the cooler and the biggest bottle of water I can find. I open the door, reach down for the container, and someone grabs my arm.

I turn around . . . "No way . . . you?"

"You mean *you*! This is crazy," Larry says, shaking his head. "Again?"

"Again . . ."

"What are you doing here?"

"Grabbing some water. You?"

"Same. Are you hitchhiking?"

"No, I'm on my bike. Are you picking up hitchhikers?"

He laughs. "Not after you, my friend. My daughters are in the car."

"Do you want me to come out and meet them?"

"Absolutely not."

"You're right. It's probably too soon."

He laughs again. "Hand me one of those, please."

"Instead of water, maybe I should get a kombucha." I ponder my choice of beverage.

"A what?"

"Look." I hold up the bottle. "It's supposed to be healthy, but it's fermented."

He eyes it suspiciously. "I'd stick with the water."

"You're right. Better not to drink and ride." I hand him the water. "You know, I've been thinking about these chance meetings. Maybe we should go to lunch and figure this whole thing out."

"I don't think I'm ready for that." Larry shakes his head. "But what do you think is going on?"

"I have no idea. Do you run into other people like this often?"

"Are you kidding?" He pauses for a moment to consider. He has a bit of a mischievous sparkle in his eye, as if he is about to say something clever. Then he raises a finger and points at me. "You know, we might need to . . . oh, my daughters . . ."

"You'd better go then."

"Okay. See you around." He goes to pay, and then heads out.

One of the young guys who works at the store stocking the shelves stops me and asks, "Was that Larry David?"

"Yes," I say. "It was."

CHAPTER 10

Can't Buy Me Love

The next morning I awake and begin to wonder if some of these chance encounters on the island are trying to tell me something. My mind drifts back again to Del Mar and meeting the Miracle. In hindsight, I feel as if the gods of love were trying to gift-wrap something wonderful for me. Yet at the time, I had my own plan: sell all my stuff, travel the world, live as a free spirit, maintain my tan, stay out of New Jersey, et cetera. Maybe if I had been less hardheaded, things with her would have worked out a lot better.

Perhaps these random encounters with Larry are leading somewhere. Since I have no career clue, maybe I should stay open to the possibility of something happening creatively. I immediately laugh this off as absurd, but then realize this thought is no more insane than meeting the girl of your dreams through a series of crazy coincidences.

I ponder all of this for a few moments. Then I think about the Miracle again and consider, *What if I had been more open back then?* Whatever the outcome might have been, it would have been a lot better than tiptoeing around my parents' house and emotionally limping around Martha's Vineyard. Let's face it—right now this stinks.

I have never thought I was inflexible, but maybe I haven't been honest with myself. This reflection makes me uncomfortable. Funny, I haven't even gotten out of bed yet, but I have taken a hell of a look in the mirror. Immediately I want to pick up the phone, call the Miracle, and confess these new insights. Throwing in an apology or two would also be a nice touch.

As the morning light sneaks through the ugly curtains, I take a look at the garage sale clock radio: nine fifteen. *Is she up?* I pick up my mobile and begin to dial her number when a piercing new thought cuts me short: *What if she's with her new boyfriend?* Then an even more disturbing one: *What if they are still in bed?*

Well, there goes my appetite, along with any sense of forgiveness I was feeling a moment ago. New thoughts arise: *Did she have to run to someone else? Why did she lie about it? If she can't be alone, maybe I wasn't so special after all.*

I hang up a few numbers short of completion. Okay, bad idea. But I do like the *idea* of being more open. I decide to begin the day with a new mantra: *I surrender everything to the divine flow. Let this be my greatest day.*

Do I actually surrender everything? Hell, no! My mind seems to always find something silly or stupid to obsess about. The difference now is I am trying to be more aware of it.

I decide to remedy this funk with a couple of shots of dark Italian-French roast, so I'm back on my bike and headed over to Espresso Love. Soon, the actress Meg Ryan sits down at the table next to me. As so often happens on this porch, conversations overlap and folks get intertwined in one another's business. Today is no exception, and soon I am chatting with Meg. I like her for a variety of reasons. She's always friendly, walks around with no makeup, and wears nappy old clothes like the rest of us summer mortals. In a way, she is the anti-movie-star movie star.

As we talk, it occurs to me that by accident, Meg had an impact on the world's burgeoning consciousness movement. Years ago she gave Oprah Winfrey a book titled *The Power of Now*, by the spiritual teacher Eckhart Tolle. This small act, in conjunction with several other factors, was part of a larger process that inspired Oprah to make Tolle's next book, *A New Earth*, the first nonfiction title ever featured by her book club. That culminated in a web event featuring *A New Earth*. The webcast enabled over thirty-five million people around the world to participate and connect.

Again, I'm reminded that some of the smallest acts we engage in can have far-reaching consequences, far beyond anything we can envision in the present moment.

A few minutes later, Billionaire Bob wanders over. To the outside observer, it probably looks like we're competing for the Outfit Most Obviously Bought at the Edgartown Thrift Store Award. Today, in a stunning upset, Bob prevails with a pair of loud multicolored plaid shorts and a fraying golf shirt with some obscure insignia partially ripped off, thus ending my thirteen-day winning streak.

It's not often you get to sit with someone like Billionaire Bob. (Actually, on this island, it's about every third day.) Our conversations always cover a lot of ground, and today we touch on politics and how finance affects the flow of things.

I toss out a question. "Why do you think the political system spins the way it does?"

"Well, the whole system follows the money. It's pretty simple: The votes follow the cash."

"Do you think it can be fixed?"

He winces a bit. "You'd need major campaign finance reform to have any chance of an honest system geared toward helping the whole, as opposed to the few. But I don't see that happening in our lifetime. There's just way too much money at stake."

"What about the economy that's in so much trouble?"

This gets him excited. "I can tell you as a guy who has started a lot of companies, we have to start creating things again. In terms of manufacturing, it's all being sent overseas because the labor over there is so cheap."

This is starting to feel too heavy for such a beautiful Vineyard morning, so I say good-bye, slap him with a quick high-five, and make my exit.

I decide to walk up to the Edgartown–West Tisbury Road and hitchhike up-island. A few cars pass me by as a giant white cloud drifts overhead in the direction of the south shore. Suddenly, along comes the vintage red Mercedes with Wall Street Mike at the wheel. Before I can even get my hand out, he pulls over. "You're turning into my chauffeur," I say. "Do you accept tips?"

"Hop in."

"What brings you to this side of the tracks?"

"I'm on my way back from competing in the Edgartown Golf Club Championship."

"How did you do?"

"Believe it or not, I'm leading after the first round."

"You're looking a lot more tan than the last time you picked me up. Did you get a job as a lifeguard?" I inquire.

"No, I'm just finding myself outside a lot. It's been much too pretty to stay indoors. Where are you headed?"

"Alley's first, and then maybe I'll grab my daily slice of pizza."

"How long do you plan to stick around on the island?"

"I'm kind of taking it a day at a time."

Mike surprises me by asking, "How are things with your father?"

"You remembered that. I'm touched."

"It reminded me a bit of my dad. We never talked much."

"He's pretty tough, but I'm trying to have some compassion. After all, the guy was practically raised by wolves."

Mike ponders this for a moment. "I wonder what my kids say about me."

"He plays too much golf and picks up hitchhikers?"

Mike smiles. "I hope that's not all they think."

"Hey, if you ever want to sell this car . . . I could never afford it."

He laughs. "Well, if I don't figure out my career thing soon enough, I might be out hitchhiking with you."

"Hey, man, two's a crowd unless there's a pretty girl."

"Speaking of which, is there a woman in your life?"

"There was . . . Or there is . . . Now there isn't . . . It's awfully complex. I'm in recovery mode these days. Actually, I'm wearing a brace under this T-shirt."

He smiles. "There's nothing wrong with taking some time off from a relationship. After all, you only got here a couple of weeks ago."

"I'm open to suggestions. You know, in the land of the blind . . ."

"Don't look to me for any help with that . . ."

Mike drops me at Alley's, and I park myself on the porch.

A ragged-looking, middle-aged woman sits down beside me. Her clothes are worn and tattered, her hair is messy, and she is talking to herself under her breath. She glares at me for a long moment, so I decide to break the ice. "How's your day going?"

"Not so good."

After a few more minutes of awkward interaction, I ask, "Where are you staying?"

"I'd rather not say."

I nod my head. "That's fine."

"Okay, if you must know, I'm living out of my car."

"Really?"

She nods.

There are homeless on the Vineyard? I shake my head. "I'm sorry." I feel a mix of sadness, sympathy, and frustration. Is there something I can do? I can't give her a place to live. It's always tough to be confronted by someone suffering and feel so helpless about it. After my silence, she continues.

"It's been a tough couple of years. They closed the plant where I was working, so I lost my health insurance. I couldn't find another job, and then I got sick. I ended up losing everything, so I came up here looking for a fresh start. It hasn't worked out too good. I had a friend who promised me a place to stay, but after a week that fell apart. I decided to hang around a few more days and see if I can get any kind of work." She pauses and gives me a funny look. "Why am I telling you all this?"

"Maybe you just needed someone to hear it."

"Maybe I did." She is quiet for a few moments. "I feel so angry. Like I screwed up or something and can't figure it out. How come this happened to me?"

"You're not alone; a whole lot of people are out of work. You can't blame yourself for getting laid off and then getting sick. I read the other day that there are something like six million people who are temporarily homeless in this country."

"Why me?"

"Sounds like you had a couple of bad breaks. But maybe you're about to turn a corner."

She gazes up into the deep blue sky and lets out a sigh. "I'm really afraid . . . and broke . . . and tired . . ."

"Times are tough. A lot of folks are scared, and I can't blame you one bit. No one is looking out for people who've lost their jobs and their health insurance."

She lowers her head, and I'm struck by the contrast between the island's affluence and her lament. America may have egalitarian aspirations, but at times our national situation feels like *The Lord of the Flies*.

"How about you?" she asks. "Do you have a home and a job?"

"No, not really. I used to."

"What happened?"

"Well, I made a bunch of money in the entertainment business, but it left me feeling empty and miserable. I was starting to hate my life, so about six years ago I walked away. I sold my house and car, and have been living off my dwindling savings ever since."

"How come you did that? You gave up a good job?" she says incredulously while leaning forward with her hands on her knees.

"I'm still trying to figure it out. The last year or two at the company, I almost felt like I was rotting inside. Like something in me that was very important was dying. I was afraid to leave, but I was even more terrified that my inner pilot light might go out and never come back on."

"Did you ever figure it out?"

"Not yet, but for the most part I'm a hell of a lot happier."

"Why?"

"That's a good question. I decided to make the life game a lot simpler to win. If I wake up and more things are working than not, it's a pretty good day. All those success gurus constantly talk about 'raising the bar.' I guess I decided to lower it."

She laughs. "I like that."

"Why make it hard to be happy? As you know, life can be tough enough. But when I think about it, I realize I've also been very lucky."

"Where do you live now? Rents are pretty expensive here."

"I'm staying with my parents, but considering my

father's mood these days, I might be better off in a car like you."

For the first time she laughs.

"Are you hungry?" I ask. "Let me buy you some lunch."

"I don't want no charity." She looks as if I've insulted her.

"Are you kidding? It's the least I can do for you listening to me ramble."

"All right then."

We go inside Alley's and pick up a tuna sandwich, potato chips, and a Coke. She digs in and says with her mouth full, "I guess I was a lot hungrier than I thought."

Near the end of our time together, I look into her eyes and try to offer a few words of comfort. "Don't give up. It could all change tomorrow."

She studies me. "Are you religious?"

This question seems to carry some weight for her, so I take a few moments to consider my answer. "I've never been a fan of organized religion, or, now that I think about it, the disorganized kind, either. How about you?"

"I used to be." She stares at me for a moment. "Will you pray with me?"

This is such a personal request that it gives me pause. Part of me is instantly resistant, probably because I am so allergic to any kind of dogma. But I don't have the heart to refuse such a plaintive plea. "Absolutely."

I hold her callused hands as she asks a hopefully benevolent God for grace. Her words and requests are simple ones as we sit with eyes closed. The joyful guests of summer move freely around us, perhaps oblivious to this spontaneous porch-front revival in their midst. Near the end of her prayer, I feel something powerful pass between us, and a tingle runs up my neck. It's hard to say which of us is more deeply moved.

I open my eyes. "Thank you." I take a crumpled twenty-dollar bill from my pocket. "Here, take it. It's all I have on me."

"I told you, I don't want no charity."

I wave her off. "Look, it's a loan. I expect you to pay me back. Consider it an investment in your future. Besides, you can't look for work on an empty stomach."

She smiles and reluctantly takes the bill. "But it's a loan, and I will pay you back."

"I know you will. Take care of yourself."

I amble along the narrow South Road for a while before a gigantic crow drops his payload right on my white shirt, thus giving credence to the age-old adage, *Let no good deed go unpunished.* In an effort to minimize the damage, I pour the contents of my water bottle on the spot and scrub it. Then, hearing a car approach, I stick out my thumb. A friendly couple in their mid-fifties pull over in a rusted-out SUV. "Where are you headed?"

"The beach."

"But you're already wet."

"I had an accident. By the way, nice ride."

"Are you housebroken? We just had this new car cleaned."

This makes me laugh. "I think I can make it all the way there. Just don't hit too many bumps."

The woman says, "We're headed to Lucy Vincent Beach. How about you?"

"That works." I look down at the water-soaked stain. "Man, that crow really got me."

"You must have deserved it," the man deadpans.

When we arrive at the Lucy Vincent, my door in the jalopy won't open from the inside, so I can't get out. They pretend like they're going to leave me in the car with the windows cracked, as if I were a dog. "Don't worry; you'll be all right. It's not too hot, and we parked in the shade. Sally, does he have any water?"

Their comedic timing is so quick, they remind me of one of those classic vaudeville acts. "So are you two comedy writers, or what?"

"No, I'm a heart surgeon," he says.

"I don't believe you."

"He really is," the woman responds and lets me out. "Dan is just a bit crazy." Ladies and gentlemen, it's the hitchhiking episode of *The Dr. Dan and Sally Comedy Hour.*

I tell them good-bye and walk down the beach to an area where swimsuits are optional. I strip down to my birthday suit and jump into the ocean. An hour later, I'm on the porch at the Chilmark Store. (Not to worry—I put my clothes back on.)

A voice calls out, "Okay, not again."

I hold up my water bottle in a mock toast. "Well, hello, Mr. David."

He keeps moving. "No time to talk . . ." He is shaking his head and laughing. "This is becoming way too strange."

"Are you having a good day?"

"I am. And you?"

"No complaints." Just to screw with him, I ask, "Which way are you headed?"

"Don't even think about it."

Larry goes into the store, then pops out a few minutes later with some items in a bag. "Have a wonderful evening."

"You too. Maybe I'll see you around."

He waves good-bye. How weird that I keep running into him.

Around sunset, I find my way back to Edgartown and sit on a bench overlooking the harbor. A handsome guy who looks like a professional athlete, with an attractive woman on his arm, asks if I can take their picture.

"You both look like movie stars."

"That's kind of you," he says, glancing at his BlackBerry.

"Hey, I'm not lying."

She wanders off to shop and leaves us to talk.

"Are you an actor or a model?"

He laughs. "No, I work on Wall Street. I'm Doug."

I introduce myself, and we shake hands. "How's the job working out?"

"Well, it's all I know. I graduated from Yale, and I've been on Wall Street ever since." He squints at his Black-Berry again, I assume checking on his next big score.

"Have you made a fortune?"

He smiles and surprises me with his candor. "I've made a few million, but I'm really a small fish. An up-and-comer." He checks his BlackBerry yet again.

"Somebody holding your kids hostage?" I ask, pointing at his smartphone.

"I have this huge real estate deal pending in Florida. I haven't slept for days."

"This might be personal, but do you feel like you have enough money?"

He laughs. "Not yet. My ultimate goal is to become a billionaire."

"Why's that?"

"If you want to be a player in the game, a billion is what it takes. That's where the real power lies. I've been a guest in the 'billionaire room,' and that's where all the important decisions happen. I figure once I'm there I can do something of value."

"So you need a billion dollars to do something worthwhile? Couldn't you make a lot happen with, say, a couple hundred million?"

Doug shakes his head at the folly of my inquiry. "No, not really. Not the big things."

"Okay. Are you happy right now with your millions?"

He thinks for a few moments and then laughs again. "No, not really. Why, what are your feelings about money?"

"It's certainly necessary, but I've always been leery of a monetary definition of success. Bruce Springsteen once said: 'Success makes life easier. It does not make living easier.'"

He nods. "Yes, that's true." Though Doug seems to be enjoying our exchange, I can tell it's also making him uncomfortable.

"Do you mind if I ask another question?"

"Go for it."

"If you're not happy with millions, what makes you think you'll be happy with billions?"

"That's a great question. I honestly don't have an answer for you." He checks his phone again, but still no deal.

"Tell me about the financial game. I'm curious; how does it work?"

"You have to be on the inside to win; it's all rigged."

Mimicking Captain Renault in *Casablanca,* I say, "I'm shocked—*shocked* to find that gambling is going on in here!"

Doug laughs and says, "They privatize the profits and socialize the losses, so whichever way the wheel spins, they win."

"How does one get into that casino?"

"You need to be in the club." His wife pulls up in a sleek black Range Rover. "I'd better go. I enjoyed it." He gets into the SUV, and I see him check his BlackBerry again.

On a purely monetary level, it sounds like a great place to be, but only if you sit on the very top of the pyramid. Still, there seems to be no correlation between material prosperity and the state of one's happiness.

Maybe, as Larry said, "Money can't make you happy, but it can make you happi*er*." Obviously the homeless lady would be better off living in a cottage as opposed to a Subaru. Would I be any less joyful with a robust bank account? No. Yet would it have eased the heartache of my breakup? No, again.

What is wealth, and how much is really enough? I don't have the answer to that question, but maybe I'll figure it out by the end of the summer.

CHAPTER 11

Bingo Tourette's Syndrome

I awake to the sound of raised voices and conclude that The Parental Asylum is again in crisis. Good God, what have I done now? Did I drink too much orange juice *again*? Under this roof, I sleep lightly and live on the edge. As official cabin scapegoat, it's always in my best interest to stay on top of these things, so I exit the bedroom and begin my investigation.

First, the facts: My parents only leave the house one night a week. Every Thursday evening, they drive over to the creaky old Veterans Hall for a couple of hours of high-stakes bingo at a dollar a game. The competition can be cutthroat, and my parents believe the game is loaded with ringers who avoid detection by disguising themselves as retired old women.

And now, back to the crisis. Apparently last night at

the hall, with no regard to the position of his markers, Dad kept yelling, "Bingo!" The other players cleared their cards, only to discover that the boy had cried wolf. Or more accurately, the wolf had cried "Bingo." The first couple of times, his fellow players were forgiving. But after repeated counterfeit outbursts, they turned on the agitator. This is frightening when you think about it; nothing is more terrifying than an angry bingo mob.

Here's the worst part: The Executive Bingo Council has decreed that if Dad can't get himself under control, he will be banned for life from his beloved hall. For life! Imagine the shame; it would be a terrible *shonda* (Yiddish for "scandal"). If, God forbid, this were to happen, my parents have decided there would be no point remaining on the island.

My father looks shaken, so I offer some solace. "Dad, it's okay." I put my hand on his shoulder. "Maybe you're suffering from Bingo Tourette's Syndrome."

"Does that really exist?"

"Apparently so. And with catastrophic consequences."

My father narrows his eyes at me. "By the way, did you finish the carton of orange juice with the added calcium? I was going to have it with the last piece of meat loaf."

When I arrived on the Vineyard at the end of June, I swear that my parents were living off an old slab of meat loaf they'd discovered behind some boxes down in the basement. I tried to save them from themselves. "You two can't eat that. You could get sick."

They shook their heads as if I was nuts. "This is fine. There aren't any bugs on it."

"That's because the bugs that tried to eat it died off within an hour or so."

"Nonsense. We can't throw this out. That would be wasteful." For the next three days, they both complained to me of stomach cramps, but had no idea how this could have happened. "Maybe we caught something from you."

"Me?"

"Yes, you. You must have given us some kind of virus."

There always has to be someone to blame. This has been a cardinal rule in our household for as long as I can remember. In fact, at one of my birthday parties, I distinctly recall a group of us kids playing a spirited game of Pin the Blame on the Donkey.

"Do you think it might have been something you ate?" This time, I refrain from specifically mentioning the meat loaf.

"That's impossible. You know how careful we are with our diet."

Yes, I do. Their diet is completely dictated by the ancient mystic god Couponishad.

The followers of Couponishad were nomadic herders who roamed about the countryside looking for really good deals on livestock, seeds, and ancient cookware. They lived by their cunning, and an absolute refusal to pay retail. When the amazing spiritual teachings called the Upanishads were released on sacred scrolls, these people vowed to wait until they came out in paperback, or were available at the ancient library.

As a lifelong devotee of Couponishad, Dad waits until the Stop & Shop coupons come out on Thursday night to determine what delicacies he will be dining on throughout the following week. As you can imagine, this leads to some—how can I spin this in a positive way—"unusual" culinary combinations.

"Wow, what's that you two are eating?" I might ask cautiously.

"A fried pork chop with Ruffles Cajun potato chips and apple-flavored Greek yogurt. Would you like some?"

"Oh, um . . . no, thank you. I ate a couple of days ago."

Luckily the lack of OJ in the fridge has not affected the sanctity of . . .

The Daily Migratory Patterns of the Paternal Grouchasaurus

- Get up and drink a pot of coffee.

  This allows Dad's enlarged prostate to awake and start harassing him into bi-hourly wind sprints to the bathroom. After his third cup and fourth flush, it's time to begin complaining about his proctologist. "How did I let that incompetent idiot talk me into that damn useless procedure?" Not that he had unrealistic expectations, but Dad believed this surgery would entirely alleviate his need to relieve his bladder. Unfortunately, he responds to any suggestion that the caffeine "might" have something to do with his urinary frequency in the same way that the Catholic Church responded to the heliocentric theories of Galileo.

- Bolt early from the house to beat the terrifying specter of traffic.

He has to pass through a treacherous area known as the Edgartown Triangle, where the Oak Bluffs and Vineyard Haven roads merge into one insanely clogged bottleneck. Though not as famous as its notorious cousin in Bermuda, it is considered by experts to be even more dangerous. Legend has it that many a moped-riding tourist has mysteriously vanished here, usually between the Fourth of July and Labor Day. Dad fears the Triangle in much the same way that swimmers fear sharks.

- Stop at the post office to pick up the mail.

If it's early in the summer, gripe about the mail not being forwarded. If later, complain about the bills arriving in the forwarded mail. His seasonal shift in negativity is one of the ways to mark the passage of time.

- Head over to the Stop & Shop and forage for supplies.

Since he rarely lets anyone accompany him to the store, his visits there remain shrouded in secrecy. To shed some light, I ask the Martha's Vineyard CSI team to run some forensic tests on his shopping paraphernalia. This is what they find: There is an abnormally high coupon-to-product ratio. The suspect only purchases items on sale. He never leaves aisle five without a box of cornflakes and two liters of Diet Pepsi. The suspect has an odd penchant for deeply discounted unclaimed birthday cakes. (HAPPY BIRTHDAY, YOLANDA!)

- Return to the safety and seclusion of The Parental Asylum.

  Dad then studies his grocery receipts like Hasidic rabbis study the Torah. He pores over them again and again until, with time, they begin to turn to dust like the ancient texts of Babylon.

After managing to successfully navigate the Edgartown Triangle, it is time for triumphant celebration and a few high-fives. The trials and travails of the two-mile round trip have left him feeling exhausted, so Dad retires to his reading chair for a long nap among his newspapers.

Between the daily trips to the grocery and the overflowing pantry closet, I assume he has the acquisition of sustenance down to a science. This makes my next observation all the more disturbing. About a week into my visit, I notice a subtle shift in his hunting and gathering patterns. After an initial smattering of the culinary offerings that I prefer, the food that I tend to eat stops showing up in the refrigerator. As a conscientious houseguest, every week I pick up the things from the market that all four of us enjoy, not forgetting to include Max. But when my chipping in doesn't alter any of Dad's buying patterns, I can't help but wonder if he is trying to starve me out.

When I casually mention this to him, Dad throws down the hospitality gauntlet. "I'm not sure why, but I don't really like having you around."

Somehow I have ended up on *Survivor Martha's Vineyard,* and just got voted off the island.

Later, Dad's personal enabler (i.e., Mom) explains, "He's upset because you don't have a job."

"After working the last ten years building up my company, you would think I'd be entitled to a little downtime. It's not like I'm asking anyone to pay my bills or anything."

Mom gives me a sympathetic look. "Your dad has the mind-set that you never walk away from work if you can get it."

"Well, I'll find something to do again. For now, I just needed a quiet place to catch my breath." I pause for a moment. "Was he always like this?"

"Oh no, not at all. We spent the first ten years of our marriage living in New York City and having fun. We ate out every night, went to shows, ball games; you name it. He was handsome and debonair—kind of a playboy, in fact. He loved nothing more than having a good time. It was a golden age for us. That was one reason why we waited ten years to have you."

"Do you ever wish you were still waiting?"

"No." She laughs. "When you came along, your father changed overnight. He became responsible; he went out, got a job at the post office, and never looked back."

"Why does he seem to feel such antipathy for me lately?"

"Dad's not mad at you. He's just had a tough life. Remember, he grew up in the Depression; he was shining shoes at the age of four. Unlike you, no one ever showed him any kindness. In fact, he once came home from the third grade and found out that his family had moved without even telling him. A neighbor had to help him find them. All of that colors everything he looks at."

I sit there and consider this. "It's still hard not to take the things he says personally."

"Never forget that your father loves you very much." Mom gets a faraway look in her eye. "Let me tell you something you probably don't know. I remember when you were a newborn. Dad came home from work while I was nursing you. He sat down next to us, began to cry, and said, 'I've never been so happy. Thank you for bringing him into my life. I love you both so much.' He loves you; he just can't show it."

A few childhood memories come to mind: *I am two and a half years old. My father lifts me up and carries me into the warm Miami water. Surrounded by my inflatable tube, I spin like a top until I drift off to sleep on the roll of the waves, safe in the awareness that Dad is close by.*

I'm five, and he takes the training wheels off my bike. I take a few nasty spills. He holds me up on my seat and whispers, "You can do it. I know you can. Ready?"

With fear and trepidation, I nod.

He pushes me along. "Pedal . . . pedal!" For a moment I am shaky; then like the Wright Brothers at Kitty Hawk I take flight on my maiden voyage. I am free.

I'm seven, and Dad and I play catch for hours. He is teaching me the subtleties of baseball; I field his grounders and catch his pop flies. Inheriting his love for the national pastime, I spend hours poring over the box scores together with him.

I'm eleven years old, and I'm being chased by the neighborhood bully. Suddenly, from out of nowhere, Dad appears and intercepts my nemesis. Confronted by an angry, six-foot-two patriarch, the villain shrinks. In a deep, growling tone, Dad conveys something menacing. The village creep never bothers me again.

I'm fifteen, and we lie awake listening to the radio. Larry King is interviewing author David Halberstam about the Brooklyn Dodgers, the beloved team of Dad's youth. Dad fills in the details: He grew up a few blocks from Ebbets Field, where the Dodgers played, and where hopelessly loyal fans were called "the bums." When he first started dating my mother, he used to take her to the games. The two of us stay up through the night sharing a love of the game.

Here's my quandary: I want to stay on the island, but I'm not sure whether 'tis nobler to suffer the slings and arrows of parental misfortune, or to take arms against my troubles elsewhere. It breaks my heart to think my father prefers not having me around. But I am kind of stuck; even though I have a nice place back in Nashville, that's the last place I want to be. It would probably take me all of five minutes to run into the Miracle with some handsome guy, laughing the night away. Yet my parents' place no longer feels safe. I feel emotionally homeless.

CHAPTER 12

Is That So?

My phone rings five times, and then goes to voicemail. A second later, it's ringing again. I check the caller ID and smile. This is a rare treat; a summons from The Great Simmons, one of my closest friends in Nashville. There are friends, and then there are brothers. The Great Simmons is the best of both. A born contrarian, he constantly pushes and challenges me to transcend life's well-worn path. We have spent countless hours developing our embryonic truths, and can easily talk through a night without any thought as to time. His wife once confided, "You two are so close, if you were a woman, I'd be seriously worried about losing my husband." Fortunately for her, he's not my type.

"How's your summer progressing?" Simmons asks. After listening to me whine about my dad, he shares an old Zen story:

A long time ago, in a small village, there lived a wise old monk named Tenzen. One day his neighbors discovered that their sixteen-year-old daughter was pregnant. Furious, the parents confronted her and demanded to know the name of the baby's father. Through tears she confessed, "It was the Zen master, Tenzen."

The parents went to Tenzen and angrily accused him of betraying their trust. "How could you do this?" they cried out. "You are going to raise this child!"

The great sage listened attentively, replying with no emotion. "Is that so?"

When the baby was born, they brought the infant to the master's door and said, "This baby is now your responsibility."

Taking the child in his arms, he replied, "Is that so?" He then compassionately cared for the newborn.

As word of the teacher's misdeeds spread throughout the countryside, he lost both his reputation and his followers. This meant nothing to him as he continued to care for the child with great love.

A year later, feeling terrible about what she had done, the young mother confessed to her parents that Tenzen was not the father. Instead, it was the young man in the butcher shop whom they had forbidden her to see. Horrified and embarrassed, the parents returned to the master's compound to seek forgiveness. "We are so sorry," they said. "We have just learned you are not the baby's father."

"Is that so?"

"With your blessing, we would like our baby back."

"Is that so?" And with that the master gently returned the child to the parents.

We conclude our conversation, and I decide that these three words—"Is that so?"—will become key to peaceful coexistence with my parents.

Suddenly feeling better about life, I go into the living room and pick up my guitar. While I am strumming and singing an old folk tune, the in-house music critic says, "You should really be a listener, not a singer."

"Is that so?" I respond to my father. Actually I can't sing that well, so he's correct on this point. *That is so!*

But I do decide that I need to let it go and not take his comments so personally. Maybe Epictetus was right: "People are disturbed not by things, but by the view which they take of them."

Another more enjoyable way in which I distract myself from my father's barbs is through one of the Vineyard's traditional summer pastimes: the daily consumption of ice cream. Fortunately for me, Edgartown is ground zero for the finest frozen dessert I have ever tasted. During the height of the season, the line at Mad Martha's on North Water Street is usually out the door. In a selfless effort to support the local economy, I never go more than a few days without indulging.

So after I finish my morning chores (feeding the chickens, slopping the hogs, baling the hay), I ride my bike down to Edgartown to pick up a cone. The beautiful smiling girl from somewhere in the Czech Republic—the one with the enlarged right arm—is generously scooping me toward my next waist size. Part of me wants to say, *Hey, that's more than enough.* But that part stays suspiciously silent.

I thank her and throw a healthy tip into a paper cup with a small handwritten note on it: TRAVEL AMERICA FUND! In between licks of mocha chocolate, I get a call from the Hollywood Birdman, who invites me to his home for a walk on the beach.

Feeling too lazy and full to bike up-island, I wander to the road in search of a lift. My first ride is with a year-round resident named Bill. I learn that apparently he's had quite a winter; he discovered that his wife was having an affair with his best friend (ouch!). Not only did this devastate him, but it also hurt his kids.

"Are you okay?" I ask.

"It's been a tough year, but I feel like I'm finally on the other side of it."

"How long were you married?"

"We met on the Vineyard ten summers ago." Bill sighs. "She got pregnant, so we decided to make a go of it. I started my own business and found myself working day and night to keep us afloat. It was a very tough time. We had two more boys, and between the kids and my new company, there was no time left for us. Eventually we grew apart, and she found her way into my buddy's arms. Lately I'm doing a lot better, and I feel like everything is going to be all right. We are working out the divorce agreement."

"I'm sorry."

"Thanks. It took me a while, but I've forgiven her."

"After everything she did? How did you forgive her?"

He takes out a small crumpled piece of paper and hands it to me. "I just kept reading this over and over."

I unravel it and read: "People are often unreasonable and self-centered. Forgive them anyway. If you are kind, people may accuse you of ulterior motives. Be kind anyway. If you are honest, people may cheat you. Be honest anyway. If you find happiness, people may be jealous. Be happy anyway. The good you do today may be forgotten tomorrow. Do good anyway. Give the world the best you have, knowing that it may never be enough. Give your best anyway. For you see, in the end, it is between you and God. It was never between you and them anyway."

"Who wrote this?"

"Mother Teresa."

"Don't you find her kind of annoying?" I joke.

He looks at me sharply.

I laugh. "I'm kidding. She amazes me; what a heart."

"That quote and the love of my kids got me through this."

We pass an open field and I think about the quote for a moment. I feel my heart slightly stir. "I heard something the other day I liked: 'Forgiveness is the fragrance that the violet sheds on the heel that has crushed it.'"

"That's beautiful. Who said that?"

"I think it was the guy at the flower shop."

He laughs. "Was that Shakespeare?"

"No, actually it was Mark Twain."

He gives me a sincere look. "Thanks for cheering me up."

"Your words are timely. My own heart feels like it has a crack in it."

"Whatever it is, you have to let it all go. For your sake, not theirs."

"Easier said than done," I reflect.

"Tell me about it. But with time, the hurting eases up, and now I'm able to look at my own part in our breakup. Besides, we all do the best we can. We're human."

Bill pulls over. "Unfortunately, this is where our roads fork."

"Thanks for the ride and the words of wisdom. That crack I spoke of feels just a little bit smaller."

He reaches out of the car window, and we shake. "Anytime, brother."

The story hit too close to home, leaving me feeling ill at ease. I stand by the side of the road trying to sort through my tangle of emotions. What was my part in the knot that the Miracle and I created? I still feel hurt by the way she handled things, especially at the end. She met this guy who was supposedly going to hire her as a sales rep. They started going to dinner, and my gut was telling me that something was off. When I asked her directly if there was something romantic between them, she denied it repeatedly. Eventually I discovered her infidelity, and I was devastated. I now understand that at that point, we were both responsible for the disintegration, but I really wish she had been more honest with me. Perhaps, like Bill, I can find forgiveness for both her and myself. (But really more for her!)

Most important, I realize that hanging on to the past is like carrying around sharp pieces of glass in your pocket. Until you get rid of them, they'll cut you every time you attempt to move forward.

I take a deep breath, and realize that I really do need to let go. I hear a car approaching and stick out my thumb. I'm surprised to see Wall Street Mike approaching yet again in his vintage red Mercedes. He pulls over the moment he catches sight of me.

I bow and say, "What great service!"

"You're welcome."

I pretend to look at an imaginary watch on my wrist. "But you're a little late."

"Sorry, I was having the car detailed for you. We don't want to disappoint."

"Should I start chipping in for gas?"

"I'll run a tab for you." He smiles.

"That's very trusting."

"I'm starting to think you're never leaving. I thought you were only staying for a week or so."

"I'm finding the Vineyard a little like the song 'Hotel California.' I can't seem to leave."

He smiles. "Just don't check out. So, where are you headed?"

"I'm meeting a new friend at his house for a walk on the beach."

He sweeps his hand across a crystal-blue sky laid out in front of us. "Well, you certainly picked a lovely day."

"It's perfect. The Vineyard seems to crank these out effortlessly. It helps me forget my own little problems." I think about my ride with Bill and my thoughts about the Miracle, and decide to venture into the realm of relationships.

"You're married, right?"

"Yes, for a long time."

"Is it tough?"

"Some days." He pauses, then adds, "Some weeks, some years . . ."

"I guess I had this naive view that two people deeply in love should move through the world peacefully, enjoying each other and calmly working things out. That there was no need to raise your voice, or be totally irrational about something that on the surface feels so insignificant."

Mike grimaces. "Maybe that's true on *Leave It to Beaver*, but not in real life."

"What about you?"

"My wife and I have had a lot of our own challenges. In fact, five years ago we almost split up. We just couldn't get along or agree on anything. For us, it was about commitment and hanging in there, even when it felt hopeless. Fortunately, we made it through the tough times, and the last three years have been fantastic. Let me tell you this: Relationships are hard work, and you both have to be willing to do some heavy lifting."

I give him a concerned look. "Exactly how much lifting are we talking about?"

"Look, wise guy, we did the work, and now we're reaping the rewards." Mike is serious about this stuff. "If you're willing to pay the price, through commitment, you'll find a way through the sand traps."

"Hey, way to work a little golf metaphor into that."

Mike agrees. "Golf is a great metaphor for relationships."

"Yes, a lot of frustration and a few good shots. By the way, thanks for the ride."

"No problem; I enjoy the company." Suddenly Mike looks a bit alarmed. "Oh no, I just realized that I can't take you all the way up-island. There's ice cream in one of those bags."

"Really, what flavor?"

"Are you serious? Cookies and cream."

"I've already had a dish of the stuff myself."

Mike shakes his head. "You seem to live on junk food and dessert."

"The Hitchhiker's Diet . . . Not many people know this, but hitchhiking is an excellent way to burn calories. In terms of cardio, I think it ranks right up there with swimming."

He laughs. "Hey, I'm sorry about the shortened ride."

I can't believe he's apologizing for doing me a favor. "No problem. I appreciate the words of wisdom. I hope I see you again."

"The next time I pick you up, I'll take you wherever you need to go. Unless it's off the island."

"Thanks, man." I smile and get out of the car.

I walk about a mile along the South Road, until I come upon the Allen Farm. Founded in 1762, it comprises a hundred glorious acres overlooking the Atlantic Ocean. Reaching a narrow and treacherous section of the road, I decide to resume hitching.

A kid in filthy overalls, driving an old pickup, pulls over. "Hop in."

Climbing into the cab, I am struck by an extremely foul odor. "What died?"

"Excuse me?"

My God, how can Pig Pen be oblivious to this nostril-numbing aroma? Alarmed, I glance back and see that his truck bed is filled with garbage. From the deadly gases drifting my way, I'm convinced at least one of those bags contains rotting fish heads. "There's a mighty strong smell coming from back there."

"I know. I need to get over to the dump and get rid of those bags. I keep forgetting."

How could anyone forget the cloud of stench engulfing this ride? Call me crazy, but even the trees are leaning away as we pass by. Turning back to Pig Pen, I ask, "Are you a freelance garbageman?"

"No, just a chef who likes to fish."

So I was right about the fish heads. I realize that he literally doesn't smell them. Isn't it amazing how easily we can get used to the things in our life that stink the foulest?

"Where are you from?" he asks.

I want to be polite, but I need to conserve air, so I merely nod.

"Excuse me? Where?"

If I take a breath to answer him, I'm certain I'll pass out. As I turn a whiter shade of pale, we mercifully arrive at the top of the Birdman's road. I get out, cough a few times, take several deep breaths, and thank Pig Pen for the ride.

CHAPTER 13

Fame and Misfortune

The path to the Hollywood Birdman's seaside estate is a meandering one with many a zig and zag, so I take my time and enjoy a leisurely walk. When I arrive, he is nowhere to be found, but I hear the sound of his voice and running water. When I locate him, he's in the outside shower, speaking on the phone. Talk about a dedicated deal maker. Birdman catches sight of me through the faded wooden slats and says, "I'll be done in a minute. Have a seat."

"Great. Actually, on second thought, it's probably a little early in our relationship for me to see you naked."

He laughs from behind the panel. "You're right. Why don't you go sit on the porch and check out the view?"

I wander over to one of his guesthouses and look out at the sea. The surf is roaring today, forcing ferocious sets of waves hurtling toward the shoreline where they will meet their demise. I reflect that the sea and shore have been doing this little dance of theirs from time immemorial; the thought makes me shake my head and smile. Light and dark, high and low, up and down, cold and hot, more or less—welcome to the world of polarity. It's all beyond me, but I love to think about it. And even though in the scheme of things I'm smaller than those infinite grains of sand along the endless beach, I'm still a part of it all. For a moment in time, all feels right in the world.

Now clothed, Birdman finds me and says, "Man, those waves are kicking it."

Breathing in the salt air, I exclaim, "God, I love that smell. There's nothing in the world like it."

"It's good for us." He looks at me, and then glances out at the ocean. "Do you realize our meeting the other day would've never happened back in the real world?"

"Really?"

"Yes. My life there is too insulated."

"So you never hang out with hitchhikers?"

"Not very often, and I'm already wondering if today is a mistake." He says this with a wink.

"Hey, I've always been curious: What's it like on the inside of the film industry?" I ask.

"The movie business is a glitzy world of surface glamour, with all kinds of serious dysfunction lurking below. Trust me, it's ugly."

"You're around a lot of people who are famous. To those of us on the outside, it looks like this fabulous party where everyone is having the time of their life. But can fame and happiness coexist?"

"I have never seen that happen. In my opinion, it's impossible to be both famous and happy."

"Why?"

"Fame is a paradigm, where fulfillment comes from the outside in. It's about the self and for the self. Period. You cannot find contentment and happiness through it. The things driving you to become famous are not the same things that will make you happy. I refer to being famous as 'the disease.'"

"But do you love your work?"

"Not really. In a year or two, I'm getting out. These days it's a lot of effort with hardly any satisfaction. Here, look at this." He lifts his shirt to reveal a series of small and varied scars scattered across his body.

"Man, it looks like you've been in a lot of knife fights."

He points to a few of the scars. "Each one of these has its own story. A back surgery here, a kidney removed there. Here's one on my neck for a vertebra."

"Wow, I'm sorry."

"Don't feel sorry for me, kid. It's the price of doing business in this world." Obviously these are his battle wounds from the stresses of a life lived in the entertainment trenches.

"Do you believe there's a mind–body connection between your scars and what you do?"

"Absolutely. This is why I need to get out—hopefully before something more serious shows up. Knock on wood."

"Did you ever love it?"

"Oh hell yes. When I started out in the business, it was all I could think about, twenty-four seven. I started in the mailroom at a large company and busted my ass. Eventually I became the guy who said yes or no on what got made.

For a while the power was intoxicating—not to mention all the money. You see, I came from nothing. My parents were blue-collar; then here I am making millions and riding around on private jets with the rich and famous."

"What happened?"

"You become jaded, the business wears you down, the people you trust stab you in the back . . ."

"It sounds brutal."

"You have no idea. And you start to build layers and walls around yourself."

I point at the scar on his neck. "And the body can start to break down."

"Absolutely. And now it's my stomach."

"What's wrong there?"

"I have no appetite. I call it man-o-rexia."

I smile.

"Follow me." We make a winding descent of a bunch of rickety wooden stairs, eventually arriving at a magnificent stretch of beach. For a moment, I envy him. I would love to live here, but then I decide it's probably not worth the suffering it would require to make that much money. Besides, I love to eat too much.

The sun is flashing off the waves, and the foaming remnants gently caress our toes. I soak up the collective majesty like a dry sponge coming out of the desert.

"Let's take the long way."

"I've got all day," I reply.

A few beats of silence ensue, and then he asks, "Hey, how's Larry?"

"We keep running into each other everywhere. It's pretty funny."

"It is a little wild; he and I laughed about it."

"What do you think about stuff like that? For instance, it's pure happenstance that we started talking and you wound up inviting me on your boat."

"It could be more than chance, in terms of your experience with running into Larry. I know people who live within five minutes of me, and I can go a whole summer or two without ever seeing them once."

"Sometimes that's a blessing."

He laughs. "You obviously know this neighborhood."

"But back to what you were saying, I wonder if synchronicity like that does occur totally by chance?"

"Can we ever know?" he asks.

"Heavens, I'm not even sure how the can opener works." I point toward the endless horizon. "And if these encounters don't happen by chance, who or what orchestrates them?"

Birdman shakes his head. "We simply cannot know. It really makes you wonder if there is a vast intelligence behind the curtain."

He continues to surprise me with his spiritual insights and his willingness to share them with me. "I find it easier to think about this stuff when I'm walking in a place this beautiful." I motion toward the scenic vista.

He nods. "The problem is, out there in 'the real world' we all get bogged down in the day-to-day crap, just trying to get through it all. We all manage to fall into a deep sleep of forgetting. I'm no exception, even here on my beach."

"We suffer from a collective spiritual dementia, where we constantly lose awareness of the ocean of magic in which we exist."

Birdman is smiling. "Precisely."

"And to think we do this while hurtling through space on a giant magnet."

"Ah, that's pretty deep."

There is a moment's pause, and then we stroll in silence for a while. I think about the Miracle, my conversation with Bill, and then break the ice with, "How can anyone be sad on such a beautiful day?"

He looks at me unguardedly, as if I am asking him that personally. "Are you pointing that toward me? It's a long story."

"I wasn't but . . ." Sensing his sorrow, I ask, "What has been the defining moment of your life?"

"Do you really want to go there?"

I shrug. "It's your call."

He sighs and looks out at the water. "When I was eighteen, my younger brother, who was sixteen, committed suicide . . ." His voice trails off. A moment of silence drifts by, as a lone osprey passes overhead. "For better or worse, it has influenced every moment of my life." I hear the pain in his voice as he continues. "My son is the same age as my brother was when he died. Crazy, no? Maybe that's why I'm too intensely involved in my boy's life. I have a tendency to micromanage his every move, which has strained our relationship."

"It's natural to be overly protective, especially after what happened. Do you blame yourself for your brother's death?"

"In many ways, yes. I feel like I should have somehow seen it coming. But I was too caught up in my own life to notice."

"You were only eighteen. How could you have known?"

"I just wish I could have done something." He shakes his head, and I feel the regret emanating from him. He looks around and adds, "Funny, I never bring anyone here."

I know he means this stretch of beach, but it could've been the dark place in his heart. We walk for a while more in silence. The stillness is eventually broken when he pulls a couple of plums from his pocket. He pauses to school me in the art of plum selection. He must know what he's doing, because this is the best one I've ever tasted.

Turning back toward his house, our roles reverse and he begins to ask the questions. "Are your parents still alive?"

"Yes. Dad is almost eighty-five, and Mom is eighty. They met at Jones Beach in New York when my mom was all of sixteen, and have been married for fifty-nine years."

"That's quite a success."

"Well, kind of. I see them more like Tony Curtis and Sidney Poitier in *The Defiant Ones*. Remember when the two prisoners who hated each other were handcuffed together in misery?"

He laughs. "Do you have any siblings?"

"Yes, a younger brother."

"Are you close?"

"We used to be extremely tight, but not so much anymore."

"What happened?"

"He married a woman who can't stop glaring at me. Since she and I have only shared about forty words in fifteen years, I'm not sure what the deal is."

He looks directly at me. "Have you asked him about it?"

"Sure, a number of times. But he just makes excuses

for her, or says I did some insignificant thing that pissed her off. After a while, I just gave up."

"Some guys do that. But don't give up. Trust me when I tell you that your brother is an important part of your life."

This makes me uncomfortable. "I'm at a loss for what to do."

"Give it some time and be patient. Is she the breadwinner in their dynamic?"

Man, this guy is sharp. "Yes. How did you know?"

"Instinct."

"She's certainly been supportive in that way. Don't get me wrong; I'm happy they have each other. It's just a shame that she is the way she is toward me, and he has never had the strength to confront her on my behalf."

"That's too bad. Again, my advice is to be patient with him and, more important, her."

"Look, my brother is a great guy. I miss him a lot . . . and never more than when I'm with him."

"You need to forgive him." A few beats of silence . . . "So, is there a woman in your life?" he asks.

"There used to be."

From our first night together, the Miracle and I are inseparable. During the two months that we stay in Del Mar, we walk along the shore daily and never miss a sunset. On one of our hikes, we see two blackbirds flying in a tight circle, rising and falling with the sea breezes.

They climb and then lock together in a free fall toward the ground, each time pulling up right before impact. This goes on for a while before

they suddenly veer off in different directions. I feel as if their aerial ac-
robatics may symbolize my dance with the Miracle. How long will we
have? I wonder. Will we share just a few weeks here at the beach, and
then part? Or will we be blessed with an all-too-brief lifetime together?

I return from my Del Mar daydream to the glory of Birdman's stretch of sand.

He smiles. "I lost you there for few minutes."

"Sorry about that." I pick up a stone and give it a long
toss into the receptive sea. "My mind caught one of those
waves back in time."

"No need to apologize; it's just us."

I put my hand on his shoulder. "Thank you."

"Well, what happened? Tell me about her."

"Here's the short version: She was a gift from God. We
had a magical couple of years. But she had stuff that freaked
me out; I was afraid to commit, and took her for granted.
She found someone else. It got ugly near the end, and I left.
Or, more honestly, I fled here."

"It sounds like you're still hurting."

"Only on days ending in *y*. Most of the time I feel
shipwrecked."

Birdman smiles and indicates the shimmering strand.
"At least you picked a good spot to be a castaway."

"How does this sound: 'Why would anyone ever want
to be married? Do we really need the Wizard of Oz to give
us state-sanctioned permission to validate our relationship?
How do you make a long-term commitment and still honor
the moment?' Impressive, huh? That was the kind of crap I
used to say to her . . . What a load of bull. I fooled myself,

but certainly not her. If I ever have another relationship, I hope I can bring a greater degree of honesty to the table. Sadly, I wasn't even aware of it at the time."

"What are you not telling me here?"

I consider his question. My initial instinct is *Nothing,* but after a few moments a wellspring of feelings comes rushing to the surface. Should I let them out here to mix freely with the sun and surf, or bury these uncomfortable vibrations that have made a run for the exit? Given the depth of Birdman's sharing, I feel as if I owe it to him to be forthcoming.

"I'm not sure where to start."

"There's no right or wrong place; just go with it."

I stumble for a beginning, but find my voice. "The power of our connection terrified me. I had never felt anything like it before. Usually I'm detached or aloof; I can walk away and be okay with it. But not this time. It was so much bigger than me. It could be like trying to bodysurf a tidal wave. The fact that she was different from me scared me, too."

"How?"

"Oh . . . she spent money like MC Hammer; the fact that she liked to drink and I don't . . . My previous girlfriend had addiction issues, so her enjoying a drink sort of freaked me out."

"That sounds pretty normal; my wife and I have tons of differences. But keep going."

"She was so illogical at times . . . It drove me nuts."

Birdman breaks into hysterics.

"What's so funny about that?"

"She's a woman, you idiot! She's supposed to be illogical!"

I shake my head. "What a mess."

"Look, there are no perfect people; only perfect opportunities."

This gives me pause. "Now that I think about it, I guess what really frightened me was a deep feeling of inadequacy. I felt clueless. That maybe I wasn't good enough for her." I pause. "Or anybody, really. I look at the dysfunction in my parents' marriage, with all its suffering. God bless them, they've done the best they could, but I really had no role models to draw from. No point of reference to go, 'Oh, that's it!' Being with the Miracle made me feel vulnerable in a way I never had before. Like being out there"—I point toward the glistening sea—"and not being able to touch the bottom."

The Birdman nods. "Well done."

"So what do I do with all that?"

"Did you tell her this?"

"I didn't even tell *me* this." I laugh. "It just came to me now. My feelings for her were so strong that there was no logic to it. And honestly, she could have done something heinous and I still would have loved this woman. Nothing could touch that love. The charge of connection and attraction was nuclear. I've tried everything in my power to run away from it, but nothing has slowed it down. Even to this day. If anything, it has only gotten stronger. I've realized that loving her isn't really up to me."

"You're lucky."

"Are you being sarcastic?"

He throws his arms up. "No, I'm dead serious. Most

people will never find anything close to that in their life-times. In fact, they don't even believe it exists."

"I never looked at it that way. I don't feel very lucky now; only broken."

His face shows concern. "Hey, you can fix this . . . trust me."

"Her love brought out the best in me and, sadly, also the worst."

"Call her up and tell her that."

"I think it's too late."

"It's never too late while you're both still breathing."

"No, I've screwed it up and killed it."

"I don't think so. Give it some thought, but I'd give her a call."

In that perfect setting I look at the Birdman and see his sincerity, hear his wisdom, and feel his compassion. "I'm grateful for that advice, and for you, I will consider it. I'd give anything to be with her again."

"You need to forgive her, and forgive yourself. It's not easy, but it's what you need to do."

"You're really a fountainhead of forgiveness today."

He breaks into a big smile. "I like the way that sounds. There will be another opportunity; you can count on it."

"You think?"

"I know." He smiles and hands me another plum.

"You're right about her and forgiving," I add. "I'll get there someday. Okay, one more thing: Has anyone ever told you how much you look like that guy in the Dos Equis beer commercials? Maybe you're the 'second most interest-ing man in the world.' "

He gives me a sarcastic look as if to say, *You're kidding.*

"Okay, here's an easy one: What *is* the key to being happy?"

"That's an easy one?"

"Since this is your home court," I say, sweeping my hand across the scene, "give it a shot."

Birdman ponders this for a moment. "You have to find your one true, authentic voice. Then live from that place."

"Like when Joseph Campbell said, 'Follow your bliss'?"

Birdman nods. "Yes. So ask yourself: What is my authentic voice? Find it, and begin there. Then, once you get ahold of it, never, ever let it go."

"Or never let *her* go . . ."

He smiles and points a finger at me. "Yes! There you go."

CHAPTER 14

I'm Robin Cook

Still buzzing from my time with the Hollywood Birdman, I leave his estate and walk up the long dirt path to the South Road. I make a right, meander for a quarter mile, and hit the Chilmark Store.

"I was hoping I'd see you again," a scratchy voice calls from the end of the porch.

A middle-aged woman is sitting on one of the rocking chairs with a half-filled cup of dark coffee. When I approach, I see that she's the homeless lady whom I met at Alley's a few days ago.

She looks up at me from under an old Boston Red Sox hat. "Do you remember me?"

"Of course I do." I gesture toward the empty seat next to her. "May I?"

"Please."

I point to her hat. "Are you a Sox fan?"

"I have been."

"Haven't you suffered enough?"

She smiles and then moves her chair closer to mine. Clasping my arm tightly, she says, "What happened with us the other day? First, I slept like a baby for the first time in years. Now, all of a sudden, I sort of feel hopeful again."

A smile slowly creeps across my face. "Really?"

"Really. But what was it? I felt something . . . electric. Did you?"

"I did feel something."

Still holding my arm, she looks me up and down curiously. "What did you do to me?"

I can't help but laugh. "It certainly wasn't anything I did." I think for a moment or two. "Maybe we reminded each other of something we had forgotten."

"What did I remind you of?"

"How we all are just a bad break or two away from hitting the bottom."

"You think so?"

"What's the old phrase—*There but for the grace of God go I*? For me, that is so true. Are you still in the car?"

"Yes, for now."

I point up the South Road. "Have you been to Aquinnah to see the clay cliffs yet?"

"No. Should I?"

"The best time is around sunset. Trust me, it's worth the extra few miles to get there."

"Then I'll go." She finally lets go of my arm. She looks past me and asks, "Do you know that guy standing there staring at you?"

I look over and break into a huge grin. "Larry."

He looks at my homeless companion and nods. "Do you know this guy?"

"Not really, but he made me feel better."

"Did you happen to pick him up hitchhiking?"

She turns to me. "Do you hitchhike?"

"Sometimes . . ."

She looks at Larry. "Did you pick him up?"

"Yes! I never do that, and I never will again." He's laughing.

I respond with, "I've been considering this; maybe I'm your guardian angel."

"Hey, don't even kid me about that. Hey, I thought you were an Edgartown guy. What are you doing way up here?"

"I just hung out with Birdman. He invited me up to his beach for a walk."

"Am I going to get another spooky text?"

"Maybe." Then I turn the tables on him. "What are *you* doing here? I read in the paper that you were in LA yesterday, speaking at a television conference."

"I was, but I just got back, and of course the first person I see is you."

We stare at each other in silence for a few moments and shake our heads. This time we have a witness. "To be honest, Larry, I got worried when I didn't see you for a couple of days."

"Very funny. I'd better get going."

"Kids in the car? Remember, you already used that excuse."

"No kids, but I have a dinner to attend."

"Speaking of eating and figuring things out . . . I'm still thinking lunch sometime?"

He shakes his head, bounces off the porch, and heads out to parts unknown. The homeless lady comments, "That was funny. Who is your friend?"

"That was Larry David."

She thinks about this for a second, then says, "Never heard of him."

"You just witnessed the 'Larry Phenomenon.' It's actually becoming quite a common occurrence."

"If it's common, how can it be a phenomenon?"

"Good point."

She smiles.

Then I say, "Well, love is everywhere, yet that's still phenomenal."

She shakes her head. "There you go again, talking crazy."

The next morning, I'm still pondering these things as I stroll through Edgartown, book in hand. It is a typical stellar summer Vineyard day: a crisp blue sky, a sprightly breeze dancing off the harbor. The birds are yammering away in the surrounding trees, which have borne witness to hundreds of years of human activity, from lamps lit by whale oil to these obnoxiously loud fossil-fuel vehicles lumbering past us. If you look closely, you can see the full moon sitting up there a mere 238,857 miles away, snoozing in its endless blue dome, catching a catnap before brilliantly coming back on duty tonight.

Much more important, it's time for a couple of shots over ice at the Espresso café. I catch a seat in the sun and slowly begin to sip my happy juice. A few moments later, an older man approaches me with his grandson. "What book is that you have?" the granddad asks.

"Richard Bach's *Illusions*. It's about the adventures of a reluctant messiah. He wrote this right after *Jonathan Livingston Seagull*."

"Oh, I remember that one. Are you by chance an author?"

"In a way, yes, but I hesitate to call myself one."

"I'm a writer, too. In fact, I just got back from China, where I was researching my next book about holistic medicine." He sticks out his hand. "I'm Robin Cook!"

Though I'm a lifelong reader, "I'm Robin Cook!" registers a zero on my Famous Author Richter Scale. Unfortunately, the blank look on my face brings him a bit of sag, confirming my suspicion that "I'm Robin Cook!" is someone I should definitely know.

In an effort to recover, I do a little emergency backpedaling. "What kind of books do you write?"

"Medical thrillers. I just finished my twenty-ninth book." Pausing for effect, he adds, "Most of them bestsellers!"

Still nothing on my end; more sag on his.

Since medical thrillers are not my genre, this last piece of information explains my ignorance. But still, I feel that I should know almost twenty-nine bestsellers and the name Robin Cook.

Unwilling to give up on the literary lacunae of the ignoramus before him, and desperate for me to realize I am in the presence of greatness, "I'm Robin Cook!" dramatically raises the stakes. "I wrote *Coma*!" (I'm sure he wanted to add, *you idiot!*)

Some inner recognition is occurring, but it hasn't reached my face yet.

He continues. "We made a movie out of it starring Michael Douglas!" (*You moron!*)

Michael Douglas? Wait a second, of course I've heard of that movie.

"It was a big hit."

Bingo! We have recognition. Making up for my earlier indifference, I respond with a tsunami of over-the-top praise. "*Coma*? Are you serious? *Coma* is one of the coolest movies ever!" Not wanting to overdo it, I stop just short of yelling, *You da man!*

"I'm Robin Cook!" is visibly ebullient, and proceeds to tell his story. "I was a naval doctor serving on a submarine when I wrote my first novel. I managed to get it published, but unfortunately no one read it. I started researching what makes a book successful, and sure enough, my second one was a bestseller."

The little boy chimes in, "Daddy, I want a dougÚut!"

Oh, so "I'm Robin Cook!" is the *father*? Shifting gears I ask, "How do you like being a dad?"

"I love it. We used to have a plane, but when we had this little guy," he says, pointing toward the boy, "we got rid of the plane."

I nod and reply, "Of course," even though I have no earthly idea what the connection could possibly be between the plane and the boy. Let me think about this. They used to have a plane . . . they had a kid . . . so they got rid of the plane . . . Beats me. But hey, I'm not about to go blank again and make "I'm Robin Cook!" explain himself again.

With my literary ignorance vanquished, Cook turns out to be quite a friendly chap. He must also be a terrific father, because his son clearly adores him. "Seeing you with your son gives me hope that I may one day be a father."

"Well, it's never too late. Look at me." He gives the boy a hug, and the affection between them touches me.

"I love kids, but everyone tells me you can't imagine how powerful the bond is between you and your own child."

"It certainly changed everything for me. Your whole perspective changes from what is best for me"—he puts his hand on his heart—"to what is best for him." He touches the little boy's head. "Trust me when I say it is worth every sacrifice."

Wow, I can really feel the love between these two. "If I'm honest, I find the whole thing rather intimidating."

"Well, you can't help but make a ton of mistakes. But if you come from a place of love, and stay on that path, everything will work itself out."

"Thank you."

"Don't miss the experience. I almost did"—he visibly shudders—"which would have been a tragic mistake."

Pointing to the two of them, I comment, "From the glow on his face, I'd say you're doing a hell of a job."

Cook gets up, shakes my hand, and moves on with his sidekick. My friend Betsy arrives just as he is strutting away.

"Who was that?" she asks.

"The author Robin Cook."

"Should I know that name?"

"Wait a minute. You don't know who Robin Cook is? Are you serious? The great Robin Cook? You have never heard of him? You're joking, right? Well, if you don't know, I'm certainly not going to be the one to tell you. You'll have to find out for yourself."

CHAPTER 15

The Magical Girl
and the Equine God

Lucy Vincent Beach (LVB) offers the finest bodysurfing on the island. The grade is flat, and the waves here are the most even. It's a private beach, so you need a pass to get on. Of course, there are charlatans like me who, through a host of tricks and shenanigans, manage to enjoy it on an illegal basis. (In a plea bargain brutally negotiated with the LVB Gestapo, I have reluctantly agreed to never publish the details of how to avoid their detection.)

I wander up-island to Lucy Vincent and down to the far side of the beach, where a coed group is playing a spirited game of nude volleyball. I decide to pass on participating, since the last time I played here, I had a ball spiked on me, which may someday affect my ability to have children.

Exhausted, I call it a day and head up to the road. A woman pulls over to pick me up, and I hop in the front seat. I immediately feel a presence behind me. Turning around, I see a young girl smiling radiantly in my direction. "Hello!"

"Hello. How old are you?"

"I'm six." She holds up six fingers. "How about you?"

"I'm old." I hold up no fingers.

The little girl smiles shyly and shows me two stuffed animals. "These are my special horses. Why do you hitchhike?"

"So I can meet people like you."

"Really?"

"Really."

"I'm on my way to the stable to ride my real pony."

"That sounds wonderful."

When the car stops to drop me off, the little girl sticks out her tiny hand, offering a handshake and the words, "Good luck finding rides." This small act touches me deeply.

I get out and wave good-bye as the SUV disappears down the dirt road. I reach for my cell phone and discover it missing. Uh-oh, it must be somewhere in that vehicle fading out of view. I really can't lose my phone. Frustrated, I set off in ambulatory pursuit.

After my marathon morning bike ride and miles of walking on the beach, did I really need more exercise? I know I'm eating a lot of pizza, but I could have skipped this part of the triathlon.

I come upon a field with two horses grazing in the distance, and pause to lean on the split-rail fence. The larger one lifts his head, lets out a whinny, and makes a beeline in my direction. Are horses territorial? I hope not. I feel an instinctive urge to run, but my body is frozen in place. The huge stallion abruptly stops a few feet from me and stares deep into my eyes. Neither of us blinks.

I find myself humbled by his mighty presence. With two steps, he closes the remaining distance between us. I gently trace my hand down his enormous neck, feeling puny and insignificant in the face of such raw power.

Heeding an invisible command, we slowly lean toward each other. He rests his head in the crest of my shoulder as I finally exhale. My hands pressed tightly against his neck, I feel the rhythmic force of his beating heart.

We share a moment of pure connection as time ceases. My eyes are closed, and for a moment I envision the smiling face of the little girl from the car. I take a deep breath; I don't want to let go.

Something mysterious is exchanged between us. We look into each other's eyes one last time, and then he snorts, wheels around, and leaves me to a world of mortal cares and trivial concerns.

CHAPTER 16

The Great Mongolian Doughnut Sage

Seeking fellowship, I make my daily stop at the town bakery, cell phone in hand. I'd walked down the long road to the stable and picked it up. Here, the man I call the Mongolian DougÚut Sage presides over his sanctum of dougÚuts and pastries. Over the course of the summer and the expansion of my waistline, the two of us have become close. The good news is, I am blessed by our fellowship; the bad news is, I can't stop by without wolfing down his dougÚuts. DougÚuts have always been my weakness. (Along with pizza, chocolate, french fries, cake, cookies, ice cream, pastries, hamburgers, hot dogs, seafood, pasta, steaks, fruit salad, candy . . .)

The Sage consistently impresses me with his wisdom and humility. He grew up in communist Mongolia, and was raised by his grandparents after his alcoholic father abandoned the family. He currently studies philosophy at the University of Berlin and journeys to the island each summer to earn some extra cash.

"Do you ever see your father?" I ask.

"No, not often. I have a love–hate relationship with the guy."

"I have that with my dad, too. I love him, and he hates me." This line gets a cheap laugh, and bonds us in a peculiar way.

"We must learn to forgive those who hurt us," the Sage intones. "No sense carrying around the deadening weight of pain."

Between the unwelcome and disruptive visits by actual paying customers, we share our take on life. For someone twenty years old, he is uncommonly deep. Though our lives began in very different worlds, we somehow ended up in the same place, sharing time and tea.

My buddy Ben walks in, notices us, and asks, "May I join you?"

"Of course you can." I gesture toward the seat.

Ben sits down with his coffee and dishes the latest island news. He's a builder, so he gets around a lot and is up on all the gossip. "Guess who I sat next to at dinner the other night?"

"Who?" replies the Sage.

"Larry David."

"Who's that?" I say, trying not to laugh.

"You don't know who Larry David is? Haven't you ever seen *Seinfeld*? Or *Curb Your Enthusiasm*?"

Like a dime-store fortune-teller I cryptically intone,

"Wait a minute . . ." I rub my chin and look skyward. "Was it . . . Thursday night? Wait . . . I'm getting something more . . . at the Atlantic?"

He looks stunned. "Yes! How did you know?"

At that moment, Mr. Flakey enters the bakery. "Do you see that guy who just walked in?" I say in an undertone, pointing across the shop. "He will claim to have lost my number, and then invite me to lunch. Watch."

Mr. Flakey wanders over and shakes everyone's hand. Then he enacts Stage Three of his charade.

Ben and the Sage look on in amazement as Mr. Flakey wanders off. Then the Sage asks, "How did you know he was going to do that?"

"My friends, I know everything that goes on in this town. Nothing of consequence eludes me." I laugh, and then share the truth.

"So you like *Seinfeld* and *Curb*?" Ben asks.

"I'm not sure yet. I plan to watch them this summer."

"You've never even watched *Seinfeld*?" Ben says. "That's impossible!"

"I'm planning to, this summer."

They both shake their heads in disbelief and disgust.

"By the way, would one of you be interested in doing a little house-sitting?" Ben asks. "A friend of mine needs someone reliable to watch his place."

The Sage declines, so I jump all over it. "This is heaven-sent. I'm sure my parents could use a break from me."

"Great. It's a little cottage right in town. I'll work things out."

It's time to celebrate, so I grab a couple of dougÚuts and walk down to the Colonial Inn. Sitting on a sofa in the lobby, I open *Illusions* and am struck by the quote "Seldom are members of your real family born under the same roof."

How true.

Looking up, I nod to a guy across from me who looks vaguely familiar. We chat for a minute before I recognize him. "You know, the world is a better place because of what you've done."

"Really? What a kind thing to say."

"What are you working on these days?"

"I just finished a film about Iraq called *Body of War*. It was a very intense experience, but it was something I had to do."

"I'll check it out."

His wife, looking as ageless as ever, breezes in and greets us warmly. "It's time to go, honey."

I say good-bye and go back to my dougÚuts.

As they walk out, I overhear Phil Donahue say, "That guy on the sofa just told me the world is a better place because of what I do." Marlo Thomas looks at him, turns back toward me, and smiles.

That night I return to Chilmark to visit Dr. Dan and his wife, Sally, who kindly invited me for dinner after we ran into each other at Lucy Vincent Beach. Their palatial home overlooks the beaches of Menemsha and Aquinnah. Dr. Dan and I take his Wrangler down to Menemsha, a quintessential New England fishing village, to pick up the main course. The dock is littered with lobster traps, fishing lines, and all kinds of other seaworthy junk. Reaching the fish market, Dan double-parks and jumps out. "Stay in the Jeep so I don't get a ticket. Oh, and try not to get into any trouble."

I watch a couple of fishing boats come and go.

"Hi!" a small voice calls to me. "Hi there! Hello!"

I look down, and staring up at me is the little girl whose mom gave me the ride the other day. She remembered me!

"Hi, how are you?"

"Enchanted!"

"I bet you are."

Her mom watches us. "You two have a special connection. She mentioned you this morning."

"Really? How nice."

Dan wanders out and asks, "How do you all know each other?"

"Hitchhiking!" comes the choral response.

"What? That's how I met him, too. And now this itinerant has me buying him lobster for dinner," he says, feigning outrage. "There's simply no justice in the world!"

Dan and I arrive back at their house, walk out on the deck, and catch the sun's last gasp before it disappears into the sea. The grounds are spectacular, with views all the way to the Elizabeth Islands. I look toward the ocean, past the expansive yard and the multitude of wildflowers. "This is truly breathtaking."

"You should get married out here on the lawn," he suggests casually.

"What makes you think I can find anyone that stupid?"

"Yeah, you're right. What was I thinking?" he says with a wink. "We always felt this was the perfect place for a wedding, but since our boys don't want to get married here, it all falls to you now." He pats me on the shoulder. "Don't let us down on this one."

"I'll do my best. I'm assuming you and Sally will be conducting the ceremony?"

"Absolutely. In fact, I'll give you away." Dan goes inside to check on dinner, then turns around. "And not soon enough."

The Miracle drifts into my thoughts. I know she would love this view, and for a moment, I wish she were here with me to share it. Recalling our happier days, a feeling of deep regret wells up within me.

I say to her ghost, "Wherever you are, I hope you are happy. You deserve nothing less." As my thoughts begin to go south, the fog creeps in and surrounds me like a moist blanket. Sally breaks me out of my morose mood with a call to dine.

Dan asks, "So, how's your summer going?"

"Thoreau once said, 'Most men lead lives of quiet desperation.' But in my case, there is nothing quiet about it."

Dan shakes his head. "I'd like for you to meet my friend Livingston Taylor. You know, James Taylor's brother? I think you guys would really click. You're both crazy in the right kind of way."

"Livingston Taylor?" I say. "He's an amazing artist in his own right. I've always loved his music. We actually met on the island twenty-three years ago."

But when we were both in our twenties, we shared a great adventure.

One morning, during the embryonic days of my hitchhiking career, I stick out my thumb and end up in Aquinnah. After a glorious day on the beach, I walk up to the road to catch a ride home. Within a minute a

truck pulls over and the driver sticks out his hand. "Hi, I'm Livingston Taylor. Hop in."

We quickly fall into an interesting conversation regarding the nature of happiness, and Livingston shares his passion for flying. "There's nothing like being up in the air. Hey, do you have time to come by my house and help me move some stuff?"

"Sure."

We end up at a seaside cabin that is more camp than palace. Stopping in front of a huge pile of junk, he says, "I'd like to move this outside."

"Great."

"Wait a minute, the hell with this crap. I say we go flying."

I can't say yes fast enough.

We pull into the airport and board his single-engine Cessna. Within moments we're up in the air and circling Fantasy Island. As the sun begins its colorful exit to the west, Livingston asks, "Hey, copilot, wanna take over?"

Speechless, I seize the controls, and soon, like the seabirds I so envy, I am flying. From my imperial vantage point, the kaleidoscope of colors and expansive views takes on a surreal quality.

My thoughts take wing to deeper places beyond the scope of the horizon and things I can see. Can I remain open to new experiences such as this? Not only here in paradise, but on the other side of that forty-five-minute ferry ride? What if I try to slow down and do less, yet experience more?

I return to the cockpit. "Livingston, it feels like heaven up here."

"Yes. We are free."

"How did I ever get so lucky?"

"We both are, my friend."

The sun has slipped below the horizon and forsaken the day. So with the encroaching darkness insisting our adventure come to an end, we reluctantly become earthbound creatures once again.

I wander back inside and join them at the table. Even with the fog, the colors in the sky are still stretching across the deep blue water.

"We thought we lost you out there." Dr. Dan takes a perfect piece of apple crumb pie off a large platter and puts it on my plate. "Save room for dessert?"

"Thank you." I nod at my plate. "I was thinking about my ex-girlfriend, and how much she would enjoy an evening like this."

Sally puts some fresh whipped cream on my dessert and asks, "Has she ever been up here?"

"No, we never were able to make it happen."

She gives me a gentle look. "Well, it's never too late."

Not one to mince words, Dan keeps it simple. "What happened?"

"The short answer is, I probably blew it."

Sally interjects, "It usually takes two to tango."

"Well, then." I take a bite of the pie and add, "I guess *we* blew it."

Sally cocks an eyebrow. "Do you think it's too late?"

Dan jumps in. "It's never too late. Get her up here. The key is to never give up." He points at Sally. "She's never thrown in the towel on me."

"The night is young, cowboy," she says with a smile. "Don't tempt me."

I consider their advice for a moment. The sun is long gone, the sky is black, and the stars are glimmering brightly. "Maybe I will."

CHAPTER 17

Nonnie-nesia

The next morning I ride my bike down to the Harbor View Hotel, a giant Victorian structure from the late 1800s. The grande dame boasts a long front porch filled with old rocking chairs, and majestic rambling gardens. This is one of the island's great vantage points, with the Edgartown Lighthouse across the marsh and Chappaquiddick Island in the distance. It also has fantastic coffee. After a couple of cups of black gold, I decide to get on my bike and burn some calories.

As I ride toward South Beach, I realize that I'm inadvertently heading straight down memory lane.

About a mile out of town, I stop beside a small stretch of nondescript woods and let the Ghost of Summers Past take me back to my aunt Joan's small cabin, The Yankee Barn, and the summer of 1974, where it all began.

Sweet Aunt Joan refuses to allow an imagination-draining television set in the cabin, forcing us to interact and create our own fun. My cousins and I play high-stakes poker for copious amounts of candy, while the grown-ups drink gin and gossip about old times.

Every evening, the entire household gathers in the darkness to listen to the CBS Mystery Theater *on the radio. Our imaginations merge into the flow of the story, and the glow of the candlelight. I lie on an overstuffed sofa with my head resting on my grandma Deedee's lap, gazing up at the high cedar ceiling as her aged hand gently strokes my hair.*

Aside from my grandmother, my best friend is the cabin's official mascot, a miniature scÚauzer named Nonnie. Though he's been written off by the rest of my family as a four-legged simpleton, I see the potential for greatness in this literal underdog. Each day I spend hours teaching him a variety of sophisticated tricks. He graciously endures my comments ("Don't eyeball me, boy!") in exchange for attention and table scraps, though not necessarily in that order. Our routine is a demanding one. We start at sunrise and end at sunset. In compliance with the local canine union, Nonnie receives regular breaks and double treats for overtime.

By nightfall, Nonnie is smarter than Lassie. Yet something is obviously amiss, for by sunrise he has completely forgotten every single lesson he so tirelessly learned the previous day. I have no choice but to make a tragic diagnosis: The poor beast is afflicted with a rare disorder—Nonnie-nesia. As news spreads of Nonnie's condition, a dark pall falls over the barn.

One afternoon I steal Nonnie's favorite old stinky slipper. Honoring our rules of engagement, he immediately gives chase. To avoid capture, I circle the sofa. It takes Nonnie only a few seconds to do the math and calculate that he lacks the speed to catch me.

Nonnie ponders his predicament, and then purposely walks away. Since he never gives up so easily, this unprecedented act of surrender confuses me. A moment later, to my utter shock, Nonnie returns with my prized baseball glove clinched between his fangs.

"Fancy a little horse tradin', human?"

Oh my God!

Then it hits me: This tiny dog, with a brain the size of a walnut, has been scamming me the whole summer. Apparently I am the naive mark being played for the fool. By "forgetting" his tricks, Nonnie continually forced us to start from scratch, thus providing himself with a daily bevy of treats. If he had "remembered" his routine, the game would have been over and there would have been no culinary windfall.

I've been had!

The whole time I was merely a pawn in his Machiavellian plot for access to the abundance of the pantry. I am obviously no match for the machinations of such a diabolical mastermind. When I realize the inferiority of my intellect in relation to this canine con man, my young ego is crushed.

After I sulk for a couple of days, a new, humbled me emerges. I vow to never underestimate the intelligence of any creature (besides man) again.

CHAPTER 18

A Tale of Two Summers

I linger by these woods savoring a few more memories of Nonnie and those innocent times: that foggy day at the wharf when I caught my first fish; the day we gathered up the courage to ride our bikes over to the haunted Dinesmore place; the summer we "borrowed" mopeds parked by the dock, got caught, and paid a hefty fine. (Never one to overreact, Mom declared that I was on my way to a life of crime.)

I get back on my bike and travel another mile down memory lane. There I turn onto a small side street and let the Ghost take me back to 1981 . . .

It was one of those hardworking yet carefree summers of youth.
The stars aligned to create a perfect storm of decadence and

debauchery: the right house, endless days of chamber-of-commerce weather, plenty of paying piano-playing work, and an ideal mix of cool roommates.

The MVY Animal House

- *In room number one, Neil and Dave, guardians of a glorious stretch of private beach where we spend our days diligently working on future cases of skin cancer.*

- *In room number two, The Artist Formerly Known as The Musinski, the ultimate lightning rod for misery and misfortune. The only thing greater than his love of humanity . . . is his hatred for people. Though The Musinski lacks the basic social skills of most people, beneath it all—I mean way, way down there . . . okay, go even a little farther . . . don't give up . . . keep going—there lives a great heart.*

- *In room number three, my brother, Chris, the hardworking farmhand, and me, the island's version of Barry Manilow.*

Chris spends long, brutal days at the mercy of the plantation's cruel overseer, nearly killing himself for a small pittance. He staggers in every night dirty and disheveled like Jim Casy from The Grapes of Wrath.

The only discernible perk of Chris's agricultural internment is a daily allotment of a dozen free eggs. These eggs, along with countless boxes of macaroni and cheese (each chemical-laden container carrying a shelf life that can only be measured in light-years), become the culinary staples of the MVY Animal House.

Sensing Chris's spirits sinking into a dark abyss, I assume the role of in-house inspirational speaker, providing regular yet obviously theoretical lectures on the virtues of hard work. These talks are usually conducted during his nightly tick-removal sessions, where like a tree monkey I carefully scan his sunburned body for any pestilence that has mistaken him for one of the farm animals.

After about a month of slave labor, Chris's prayers are answered when he is summarily fired from the farm for reasons that to this day have never been properly explained. On the positive side, the MVY Animal House's collective cholesterol levels immediately drop 68 percent.

Returning to the vocational casino, Chris once again rolls snake eyes, winning a dishwashing job at a local restaurant. Ten hours a day he toils at the mercy of two highly creative sadists whose primary goal is to destroy their employees' will to live. For some strange reason, my brother finds working in an extremely confining space—while doing heavy lifting in 120-degree heat with steam blasting his aching body as the hostile proprietors yell obscenities at him—not to his liking.

Go figure.

Unfortunately, Chris's career as a Hobart tecÚician proves to be about as financially rewarding as his previous role as feudal serf. Somewhere his dream of a fun and carefree summer has gone horribly awry.

Since my coffers are overflowing with coin from a steady stream of high-paying piano jobs, I encourage my brother to resign from the hospitality industry and spend the rest of the summer in recovery on my fraternal payroll.

One evening under a full moon on the virgin sands of South Beach, a few yards from the crashing sea, on top of a nasty old sleeping bag, for *the first time, I participate in life's oldest dance. With the beaming moon lurking over our shoulders, my girl and I undulate like the nearby waves. Primal passion overtakes us as we become lost in the ecstasy of human renewal.*

Afterward, I feel as if I am looking at the world with newborn eyes. In the sensual afterglow of the moment, it occurs to me that every person who has ever walked the earth has arrived here through this ancient act.

The state of my chastity isn't the only thing altered that evening; that old sleeping bag is transformed as well. It is henceforth christened "The Shroud," and we in the house decide that it has supernatural powers to seduce the opposite sex. By August, with its conquests piling up, The Shroud begins to achieve mythic status.

This track record is rendered all the more impressive, given its aroma. To put it bluntly, The Shroud reeks.

Unfortunately, in an act of unimaginable negligence, upon my departure for my final year in college, I leave The Shroud in the care of the household. (Oh, the folly of youth.) What was I thinking?

As legend has it, The Shroud spent years wandering in the desert, and even spent time with a popular entertainer in Las Vegas. It eventually wound up at a fraternity house in the Northeast, where one night under a luminous full moon, it magically ascended, never to be seen again.

CHAPTER 19

Not My Day to Die

I release my regrets surrounding The Shroud and continue my ride toward the beach. Cruising past an open field of farmland, I wonder how this vast expanse of landscape has evaded the developer's grasp. Fortunately for all of us, the people of the Vineyard have been vigilant in protecting the island. There was practically blood spilled when the McDonald's Corporation had the audacity to propose an Edgartown franchise. I'm grateful that somehow, in the devastating era of the bulldozer, the Vineyard has managed to stay so pristine.

As I reach the coast, I park my bike and walk out onto the soft sand of the Right Fork Beach. Of course the Ghost would bring me here. As the tide rolls in, my thoughts drift back to the summer of 1987 . . .

I am living in "Lost" Angeles, where everyone else is rich and successful, while the twenty-six-year-old me can't even get arrested. I throw
my hat in the ring for any job in the entertainment business from music
to film, but I cannot seem to land a gig. I am always a day late, the
second to last guy not chosen, overqualified, under the radar, too aggres-
sive, or in some undefined way not the right choice. Can I manage tal-
ent, be an agent, run an errand? I keep saying yes, but the town keeps
saying no.

Absolutely nothing clicks, and I find myself struggling with depression. I begin to question my existence. Why am I here? Is my presence
relevant? Does my meaningless little life matter? As my pain grows
deeper, my Vineyard homing device kicks in and I instinctively return to
the island. In a bit of good fortune, my brother, Chris, decides to join me.

One brilliant August day, we wander down to the Right Fork
Beach to ride a few waves. The surf is raging and the riptide is fierce, so
the wiser sun worshipers, including Chris, prudently stay out of the
water. Being a strong swimmer, I arrogantly dive in and tempt fate.

It takes my hubris only a couple of minutes to realize the water has
a will of its own. I attempt to swim laterally out of the rip, but this invisible river will have none of it. Undeterred, I kick into high gear and
begin to fight the malevolent force.

After a few minutes, I look around and realize that the current has
already pulled me a fair distance from shore. Though giving it my all,
I'm no match for this massive tidal beast dragging me toward oblivion.
My body begins to cramp, and with no one close by to assist, my inner
warning lights begin to flash code-red. I have an alarming thought: On
this sparkling day, a couple hundred yards from the safety of the shore, I
could die.

My primal survival mechanism screams in defiance, NO! I'm not going to die today. I refuse to drown. I will live!

A silent voice from a timeless, peaceful place within me emerges, and something snaps. I suddenly feel a strange detachment from the fellow in the water struggling to survive. The voice begins to speak . . . This is my moment of transition.

The person in the water silently replies, Why here and now? I never got to say good-bye to everyone. This does not seem fair!

How majestic this moment is. Don't fight; just go with it.

I can't give up. This cannot happen to me. I'm not going to die!

In my struggle to survive, my thoughts cover a lot more ground than my breaststrokes. I begin to run out of energy. Where is Chris? I have to see my brother one more time. I can't leave him here alone. There he is sleeping peacefully on the sand. I love you, Chris!

The last of my will fades, and I begin to rapidly expand out of myself. I can hardly feel my body now. How strange to die. What is this peace? Funny, I do not have any fear. Why?

Time bends, and I'm suddenly ten years old and back in the Everglades National Park. I see the tall grass swaying, feel the gentle breezes blowing across my face, and watch as a deer nurses her newborn fawn. The peace I experienced that day feels like this.

It was there all the time.

I viscerally experience other memories equally as profound . . . the smile of a stranger, a shooting star, the view from the mountaintop, my dog's heartbeat, and one particular extended embrace . . . These were my moments of authentic connection, when the superficial layers of life dropped away.

All of that exists now in this moment.

My body's struggle winds down to stillness, and I begin to feel bliss. Everything is as it should be.

I feel a moment of regret that my actions ever hurt anyone. Yet see that it was merely the result of my own ignorance.

There is Grace. Unimaginable Grace.

What comes next? Inwardly, I laugh at the absurdity of the question, and let go even further.

There is no need to know . . . anything.

I am finally at peace.

There is so much love.

Thank you. Until now, I was never sure I believed in God, yet I always felt connected to something.

Yes.

I realize whatever It is . . . It is ineffable. It exists far beyond words, labels, and understanding.

Nothing matters, yet everything is sacred.

How perfect. Good-bye, world.

"Hey!"

Am I dreaming?

"Are you okay? Do you need help?"

These invasive cries startle me from my tranquil descent into the depths of being. I wearily look back at the open sea to discover two women on a single surfboard paddling toward me. I find one last vestige of will within and shout, "Yes! Help!" My tank hits empty, and I start to sink below the surface.

One of the girls jumps off the board and cuts through the water like a motorboat. She reaches me and manages to hold me up until the other girl arrives on the board. With their help, I climb on, and the three of us paddle slowly to the shore, where we are met by a team of lifeguards.

I'm pulled from the water and collapse into the warm, welcoming arms of the sand. I lie there for a while as waves of relief wash over me.

For reasons I don't know, this was not my day to die.

Later, I wander down the beach to find the two angels who divinely intervened. "Thank you for saving my life."

"You're welcome. We're here to help each other."

I nod meekly. I say good-bye, still in a state of shock, and walk away. Something within me has shifted. I feel changed, but not in a way I really understand.

A while later, I leave the island. In the next few weeks, ancient wisdom and new friends arrive on a daily basis. Conversations with people I meet fertilize my expanding awareness. I keep running into teachers: an illuminating book, an enlightening lecture, a class on meditation.

One evening while reading a book about miracles, I am suddenly taken back to the Right Fork Beach and my incredible rescue. I realize that the two girls showed up right in the nick of time; one minute later, and I would have drowned.

Suddenly I'm on my knees, the tears flowing freely. They come in an ethereal mix of joy and gratitude.

I say to no one in particular, "Why me?"

A timeless voice within me replies, "Why NOT you?"

"Why do you care about me?"

"How could I not?"

"Do you play favorites?"

"Not in the way you might think."

"Is life better than death?"

"Life and death are two sides of the same coin. Neither is better or worse."

"Can we ever understand these things?"

"Only your heart can know. What matters most is invisible to the naked eye."

Eventually, I fall asleep. From that point on, I feel like part of me is living on borrowed time. Like my number was called, but when I got to the front desk to turn in my body, they said, "Oh, never mind, we will come get you later."

Having dodged a bullet, or more accurately an undertow, I literally have a new lease on life. What should I do now that my stay has been extended? I'm not sure, but I do know that I want to become a little more conscious and maybe not take so many of the little things so seriously. When I was sinking out there in the surf, it became blatantly obvious that 99.9 percent of what I thought mattered was irrelevant. Of course I forget this all the time, but never for quite as long as I did before.

This brush with my mortality, definitely for better than for worse, sticks with me.

CHAPTER 20

The Ancient Gods of Love

It's a new day, and my plan is to take the seaside bike path to Oak Bluffs. When it comes to my sense of direction, I'm more Magoo than Magellan. I usually end up lost. Luckily, on an island, you can't get too far off-course.

There are endless miles of dirt roads on the Vineyard, and I often turn randomly down these streets to see where my tires take me, eschewing the well-worn route for the bike path less traveled.

So today, at the fork in the road, I follow a feeling and change direction. I head through the state forest and wander through her inner confines. Looking up, I see a solitary hawk making lazy circles above me. I have no idea where I am, but it's just too pretty for me to be concerned. In a fitting metaphor for my summer, I realize I'm not lost; I'm just exploring.

I eventually pop out somewhere in West Tisbury. The town is basically a couple of buildings, the Agricultural Hall, and Alley's store. The rest of it is rambling green space, extensive stone walls, and miles of hidden beaches. I stop at Alley's for a bottle of water, and since my legs feel tired, I decide to ditch the bike and travel by thumb. An elderly couple in an old Chevy pulls over, and the man behind the wheel asks, "Where are you headed?"

"Lucy Vincent Beach for a swim."

"Hop in."

As I climb in the back, I notice they are holding hands. Ah, lovebirds. "How long have you two been together?"

"Sixty-four years," he says. "I met her when she was all of seventeen, and I was a spunky nineteen." He turns toward her. "It feels like yesterday, doesn't it?" She nods.

"So, what's the secret? How do you make it last? I mean intimacy, not longevity, because some wars last more than a hundred years."

She goes first. "I think it comes down to forgiving the other person and having a short memory."

Then he chimes in. "Sacrificing and not putting yourself first. On top of that, I say yes to everything she wants." He laughs.

She gives him a playful slap on the arm and says, "He has always been a wise guy."

"We love being together, whether it's just taking a drive or grabbing a bite. Plus, she puts up with me, and that's not an easy thing to do."

She's still pondering my question. "It also takes a sense of humor—that's a big one!"

He nods in agreement. "You can't take yourself too seriously; you have to be able to laugh at yourself. Relationships are work, but the payoff is worth it. It's not easy, but it doesn't have to be hard. Most of all, I got very lucky with her."

I ask, "Have you heard the Greek proverb that says, *A heart that loves is always young*? Whatever it is, you two have surely found it. I hope I can do the same someday."

"Thank you," he says modestly. "We did, and you will, too. Just stay open, because you never know when magic might happen."

His words hit me between the eyes: *You never know when magic might happen.* I sit in the backseat and ponder this mantra. Although they look like common working folks, through their love they have found something quite uncommon. Seeing them together is inspiring.

We reach the road to Lucy Vincent Beach, and the old rig pulls over. They wave good-bye and drive off, still holding hands. I wonder how much time they will have. How will the one left behind cope with being alone? I hope they leave this world together, like one of those old washer-and-dryer sets that wear out in the same week. If love does survive beyond our mortal forms, these two souls will never be far apart.

At one time, I had envisioned the Miracle and I growing old together. I recall how compatible we were before things got so rocky. There were so many little things that at the time seemed completely insignificant, but

now in hindsight feel like tiny jewels. Like the way she would always come into my home office and gently begin to close down my laptop with the words, "Okay, that is enough worldly events for one day. You've been up here for hours. It's time to close up that portion of your brain and come with me for a long, relaxing hike."

Of course I would plead for just a few more minutes. "Hey wait, just let me finish this last article on the Middle East." But she would close the portal down.

We would then go for a stroll through the deep woods surrounding the house, our three mixed-breed rescue dogs running ahead of us, courageously clearing the path of any imagined danger lurking behind a tree.

I'm not even sure what we talked about, but we always seemed to have something to share. At some point she would always declare, "You know what I want to do tonight?"

I absolutely knew what was coming but I pretended to be clueless. "What? Clean out our closets?"

"Get a movie and curl up on the couch under the blanket with you. And I get to pick the film."

This surely meant watching some B-grade chick flick with every cliché known to man. I might in vain suggest something foreign, or that new George Clooney movie with dark political overtones, but that idea would be instantly vetoed by the Miracle Movie Committee of one. Our film would be followed by some time in the hot tub, a long snuggle, whispered conversation, and passionate lovemaking.

I would always wake up first and wander downstairs to begin construction on our lattes. The Miracle was famous for her morning grouchiness, and only my potent combination of espresso, cream, and sugar could remedy this condition.

Again, it was these small rituals and patterns that made me miss her most. I liked taking care of her, paying the bills, making the coffee, being called on my shit, and building something together.

In retrospect, what else matters?

Still, I was never all the way in, because I was so afraid of being hurt. Yet ironically, my fear ended up creating just that—intense loneliness and pain.

Suddenly I have to talk to her. I fish out my phone and dial the Miracle.

"Hello?" Just hearing her voice opens up a part of me that no one else can touch.

"I wanted to let you know I was thinking about you."

"How strange that you called," she says. "I have been thinking about you a lot."

"Really?"

"Yes, and what a pain in the ass you can be." There is a pause, and then she bursts into laughter.

I laugh, too. "Hey, don't mince words, now. Tell it to me straight."

She is quiet for a moment. "You *are* a pain in the ass, but so am I. We all can be. But you are definitely way worse than me."

"I certainly can't argue with that."

"You're awfully agreeable today."

"I've probably spent too much time in the sun."

"God, there's so many things I have wanted to tell you, to bounce off you. I miss our friendship."

"I know what you mean."

"The other night I was with some friends, and something happened that only you would have completely understood. I tried to explain it, but no one quite knew what I meant."

"The value of shared history."

"Yes. Then on the drive home I was so mad at you."

"For what?"

"Everything! And nothing at all." She laughs again. "And at how stupid we were, how stupid we still are, all the petty stuff. Our egos trying to be right. None of that stuff mattered."

"I miss a lot of the simplest of things. The day-to-day, checking in, sharing a meal or a dessert . . ."

"Yeah, but you always ate way more than me. I should have gotten my own dessert."

"Live and learn. Hey, I was only trying to save you the calories."

"Oh, that's a good one. I was always complaining about my weight." She pauses. "But I felt beautiful when I was with you. You made me feel beautiful . . . and understood. You got me. No one else gets me. It's lonely."

There is a long silence as I soak all this in.

Then she says, "Are you there?"

"Yes. I was just thinking about what you said. You were right. It's been hard."

"Even there?"

"If only geography could cure heartache."

"Or ice cream . . ."

"Actually, ice cream does cure heartbreak. If you choose the right combinations of flavors."

She laughs. "Well, you could always make me laugh."

"And piss you off."

"Yes, but you made me laugh more. Are you still living with your parents?"

Now I laugh. "No, it was time for me to move out—kind of like a mercy killing."

"Now, that's funny."

"I have a small room at a friend's house right in town. It's modest, and peaceful for the most part, although the people there also watch a lot of television. I guess I'll be forever cursed by the blaring presence of the dim blue light."

"That must be your punishment for blowing it with me."

"I wish that was the extent of it. That would feel like a slap on the wrist."

She sighs, "Oh, Pauley."

There is a moment or two of silence. Then it just comes out of me. "I still love you, you know."

Silence.

"I love you, too, Pauley."

CHAPTER 21

The Ted Danson Principle

The Edgartown Yacht Club represents a great bastion of WASP tradition. As a longtime closet sociologist, I enjoy watching the navy-blazered blue bloods march down Main Street to the insulated social safety of their own kind. (They may march down, but after a long night at the bar they usually stagger back.)

This morning I'm at the Espresso talking with Wendy, whom I've known for years through mutual friends, and with whom I've played tennis. She looks like she was conceived, born, and bred at the club: white hair, blue eyes, tall and lean—the ultimate Aryan prototype. But if you talk to her for five minutes, you quickly discover her soul is distinctly blue-collar. Three years ago, I shared my idea for a TV show with Wendy and she said, "You should meet my cousin, Ted Danson. You know, the actor from

Cheers? I have a feeling he would be interested in your concept."

I started to pin all my hopes for the project's success on my savior Ted, and why not? Ted is smart, progressive, and connected; he would be *perfect* for this project of mine. Surely if we met, everything would fall into place. As it turns out, however, Wendy, try as she may, is unable to hook us up. Ted is either too busy, out of town, not calling back, only here for a weekend, or unavailable. Wendy keeps apologizing, but I tell her not to worry—sooner or later it will happen.

This year, at the beginning of the summer, I see Ted, accompanied by his charming wife, Mary, at Alley's. I go up and introduce myself as a friend of his cousin's, and we chat pleasantly for a few minutes. Yet something about our encounter feels off. It takes me a while to figure it out: I've always felt uncomfortable approaching others with an underlying agenda. I know we all do this to varying degrees, but I feel better when I meet someone without a pretext.

So while a part of me was excited to see Ted, another part feels disappointed with myself. Have I joined the ranks of those who look to the famous for fulfillment? Today, we worship fame in the same way that people used to admire virtue. The celebrities of today resemble the saints of medieval times. So we mortals wish to get as close to them as possible, hoping that some of their special aura will rub off on us, thus transforming our lives of mediocrity into something magical.

I run into Wendy again, and mention my encounter earlier in the week with her famous cousin. "Great. I'll call him and get you guys together. I have always felt like the two of you would really click."

A couple of weeks go by, and nothing happens. Wendy acts uncomfortable the next time we see each other. That's right, it's The Famous Cousin Lean-back.

Disappointed, I try to let the whole Savior Ted thing go and give up on my hopes for celebrity salvation.

One bright August day, I ride my bike to Alley's for a cup of coffee and the mandatory pastry. I come upon Birdman perched on the porch, zealously pecking away at a calzone.

He throws up his hands and says, "You again!"

"You can run, but you cannot hide."

"I've got to get home. Do you want a ride, or is it more fun to hitch with the rich and famous?"

"I'll cheat and take the lift," I say, hopping into his convertible. "Can you drop me at the Chilmark Store?"

"Pizza?"

"I'm addicted." With the top down, we ride along, catching up on all the insider island scoop. "How are the three kids?"

"Busy, sunburned, rebellious, exhausted."

"Sounds normal."

"Have you talked to your girl?"

"I have. Thanks for asking."

"Is she coming to see you?"

"I haven't gotten that far."

"Don't let fear stop you."

"By the way, thanks for your friendship this summer. It's meant a lot to me."

"It's much too early for me to be sentimental."

"Duly noted." We shake hands as the car comes to a stop.

I get out and walk straight into the warm smile of Ted, who may have seen me exiting Birdman's car, thus giving me an invisible seal of approval. We exchange greetings, and keeping my priorities in order—(1) Pizza, (2) Famous People—I go inside to get my piece of the pie.

When I return to the porch, Ted surprises me. "Are you on your own today?"

"Yes, I am. Are you?"

"Yes, Mary's out of town. Would you like to join me for lunch?"

"I would love to." (The big meeting at last!)

Midway through our meal and an easy flow of small talk, I realize there is no agenda lurking in my back pocket. I'm just here with a great guy, on a gorgeous day, sharing an interesting conversation. Stripped of any expectations, our encounter unfolds organically. And why should our inter-action be any different? Because Savior Ted happens to be on TV? Is that what matters most? Does fame or celebrity give a human being more inherent value?

Ted is comfortable in his skin, and exudes warmth.

Ted Danson Highlights

- He accidentally fell into acting at Stanford, and feels that he got lucky in his career.

- He still loves what he does.

- He met his wife, Mary, when he
  auditioned for the film *Cross Creek*.
  Though he didn't get a part in the movie,
  a friendship began that led to something
  extraordinary.

- She is the best thing that ever happened
  to him.

- He loves the Vineyard because there are
  no high-speed auto chases.

Near the end of our meal, he asks, "What are you up to?"

"I'm kind of between ideas right now. The last couple of years have been my time in the vocational desert. But being on the island this summer has helped clear my head."

Ted ponders this for a moment. "Sometimes we need to step back from everything for a while, to have a better sense of who we are and what path we want to take."

"I know, but the not knowing can be hard."

"Don't worry. You're going to be all right."

"Thanks for that." I stick out my hand and shake. "That was generous."

He waves it off. "Ah, don't worry about it." He motions to the clear sky. "Well, it's too beautiful a day to be here in the shade."

And with that, he gets up and departs.

As we say good-bye, I officially remove the moniker *My Savior* from the ever-gracious Ted.

Walking along the water at Lucy Vincent Beach, I realize how different my relationships would be if I just allowed everyone to show up and be who they truly are. What if I just let them simply shine their light, unencumbered by the crippling weight of my projections?

From now on, I will not contort my view of others to serve my imaginary needs. I christen this new paradigm *The Ted Danson Principle*.

CHAPTER 22

Mother Nature's Son

I usually start each day with a ride along the beach road bike path from Edgartown to Oak Bluffs, and this morning is no exception. On the fourteen-mile round trip, I am surrounded by water, with the Atlantic Ocean on one side, and the sprawling Sengekontacket Pond on the other. The pond is also home to the Felix Neck Bird Sanctuary, so the skies are always filled with spectacular aerial traffic.

I pass a few holes of the Farm Neck golf course, and then come upon the Polar Bear Club gathering for a swim at the Inkwell Beach. For generations, Oak Bluffs' large African American population has come to this hundred-yard stretch of beach to congregate and catch up. The town features an array of multicolored gingerbread houses lining an area called The Campground, with an open-air tabernacle that was built in 1879. Oak Bluffs is also home to the oldest operating platform carousel in the world, the Flying Horses.

After a long ride along the coast, I park my bike back in Edgartown and solicit a ride. After a couple of minutes, a woman about my age stops and picks me up. I discover that she is an international water expert, and I receive a crash course on the world's coming water shortages. Her critical point: "Even if we take immediate action, disaster is inevitable."

"There's no hope?"

"Not really. There will be huge, catastrophic changes over the coming years. Water, not oil, will be the first major resource in crisis."

"Gee, nothing like a little light conversation to start my day."

"Sorry about that."

"Can I ask you a favor?"

"Sure."

"Do you mind dropping me off in front of the hardware store? I want to buy a rope to hang myself."

"Very funny. How about Alley's?" The car pulls over.

"Thanks for the ride."

"Sure. Have a great day."

I grab some lunch at Alley's, and sit on the porch next to a young woman who recently interned on a research ship traveling from Hawaii to California. "Did you enjoy it?" I ask.

"It was life changing."

"Why?"

"There were a lot of amazing moments, but passing

through a garbage island the size of Texas was completely mind blowing."

"Texas?" I repeat in disbelief.

"Yes. It was gigantic, and filled with all kinds of crap. Floating chairs, toys, plastic, and things I won't mention since you're eating your lunch. Tons of floating garbage stuck together in the middle of the Pacific Ocean, the size of Texas. It was surreal and depressing."

I repeat in disbelief again, "Texas?"

All of this bad news takes away my appetite, so I tuck my half-eaten sandwich into my backpack and depart.

After receiving these two devastating environmental updates, I decide to seek refuge at the far end of Lucy Vincent Beach. I gaze at the dunes, formed by their timeless dance with the wind, and let the sun warm my face. When I jump into the surf, nature rewards me with row upon row of perfect breakers.

Looking toward the horizon, I find myself swimming with a couple of seals. In all my years in the water, this is a first, so I discreetly try to get as close to them as possible. (Kind of like I did with Mary and Ted.) Every now and then, the seals stop and stare back at me. Maybe I'm projecting, but we appear to look upon each other with a shared sense of curiosity, though God only knows what they think. *Who is this strange, poorly designed creature sharing our habitat?*

I stop for a moment and take stock of my surroundings, which call to mind a statement by Confucius: "Always and in everything let there be reverence." On days like this, it's easy. The sun is shining brightly in an almost cloudless sky, and I'm struck by how exquisite this moment feels. How fortunate I am to simply bask in this glory, like my shiny black swimming buddies and the seagulls on the shore rifling through my backpack in search of my sandwich.

The gulls finish my leftovers and let out a shrill cry, which I interpret as a gesture of gratitude.

You're welcome!

CHAPTER 23

The Lucky One

That evening, some longtime Vineyard friends invite me to a clambake at a huge estate on the south shore, miles away from the pedestrian folks who live in normally proportioned homes. I chat for a few minutes with the hosts, meet a few new people, chow down on a bunch of gigantic shrimp, and then wander outside. Cool night air cascades off the Atlantic Ocean and catches up to me on a remote stretch of unspoiled beach.

I'm seated before a roaring bonfire, staring into the shifting embers. I reflect that an open fire under the stars is such a rare occurrence in our lives today. Most of us sit trapped in towers with sealed windows in an anonymous row of dehumanizing cubicles. A somnolent hive of drones, we diligently burn away our precious lives on work that has no connection to our souls. We've become a standing—or more accurately a seated—army of medicated slaves, wasting away in search of Madison Avenue's abstract idea of success.

I decide to get up and move around. I take a marathon walk along the ocean's edge, and eventually collapse into the dunes. I remember a night like this that I shared with the Miracle . . .

It is a winter evening in Nashville, and the Miracle and I sit in the hot tub on the back deck. The water is a welcoming 110 degrees. Snow covers the ground, and the temperature hovers near zero. Andrea Bocelli's magnificent tenor serenades us from the speakers in our bedroom. A million distant pinpricks of light fill the night sky. Miracle's bare back is pressed against me, my arms wrapped tightly around her lush form.

Suddenly, just off the porch, something stirs. We turn to see two voyeuristic deer standing close enough to splash. They look like they're about to jump in with us. Miracle laughs at their expressions, and the deer turn as one and disappear.

"I'm ready to get out." The Miracle stands up in all her naked hot sexy glory. "Are you coming?"

"It's so beautiful, I might stay in here a few more minutes. How can you leave a night like this?"

"That's too bad, because I may be sound asleep by then, and I would so like you to dry me off."

"As I was saying, I think the worst thing you can do is stay in the water too long. It really dries you out."

We both laugh, and then wander inside for a passionate embrace.

The next afternoon, I'm at an Edgartown cocktail party awash in blue blazers, deep tans, and inane small talk. These folks haul around their genealogy papers like most of us carry our driver's licenses. At least the food is sensational. In case you end up trapped at one of these stuffy affairs, here are a few tips:

Edgartown Cocktail Party Helpful Hints

- Order a gin and tonic—the signature drink for Those Who Belong.

- Pretend the waiters are invisible.

- Never interact with someone new. What would be the point?

- Guys, go with the blue blazer and khaki slacks. Tan pants if you want to really shake it up. Always keep one hand in your pocket and nod a lot.

- Gals, wait until she walks away, *then* begin to gossip about her.

- Throw your head back and laugh dramatically at the stale old jokes.

- You should have recently been in the sun, preferably sailing.

Which leads us to our next section: acceptable subjects of conversation. If these subjects cover too much ground, narrow it down to the select few you feel most comfortable with.

Edgartown Cocktail Party Acceptable Topics of Conversation

- Sailing.

- Will the weather be suitable for sailing?

- What happened the last time you went sailing?

- Describe your expensive sailboat that you are refurbishing.

- Any sentence with the word *spinnaker* in it.

- Recall your glory days with the sailing team at boarding school.

- Wistfully wish you were out on the water right now.

I leave the party and walk a mile to the Edgartown Post Office to mail a letter. Feeling lazy, I decide to hitch back to town. A battered Ford Explorer pulls over, and I immediately recognize the driver.

"Where are you headed?" he inquires.

"Back to town. How about you?"

"I'm just running some errands."

"Mind if I tag along?"

"Are you sure? You'd probably be bored."

"It would be nice to spend some time with you."

"Okay. Can you believe this heat? We should have gotten a place in Canada."

"Yes, Dad, you should have. How come it always gets so hot in August?"

I should take a moment here to point out the parameters of Dad's comfortable climate window. The temperature should be between seventy and seventy-two degrees, the humidity at 43 percent, no clouds in the sky, barometric pressure holding steady, with a light sea breeze. Anything outside of this zone makes him irritable and warrants complaining. It also inspires talk of preferable places to live with more suitable biospheres: Canada, Miami Beach, San Francisco, North Carolina, Las Vegas . . . Of course, for this system to work, Dad would have to own at least one home for every month of the year.

As we drive around town, I notice his hands on the steering wheel. My father has soft, beautiful hands with weathered lines. I imagine those hands holding me as a baby.

Baseball has always been a touchstone for us, so I revert to our familiar theme. "Can you believe the Red Sox?"

"Take it from an old Dodgers fan, the heartaches never end. Boy, the island is packed. They should limit the number of cars they allow on the ferry." Another familiar refrain.

I fulfill my portion of the ritual and say, "I know, they should."

"How's your place in town working out?"

"Actually quite well. It's small, but it's all I really need. The price is right: It's free."

"Are you taking care of yourself?"

"Yes and no. Despite my appearance I haven't gone

completely feral. A friend works down at the bakery, and he's always plying me with free dougÚuts. Eating must be my calling."

He laughs. "You don't look like you've put on any weight."

"If I wasn't riding my bike all over the island, I'd be visible from space. This has been a great summer for indulging my passions."

"Are you still doing a lot of hitchhiking?"

"All the time. It's a great way to meet interesting people."

"Maybe Larry David will pick you up again."

"I doubt it. Not after all the questions I asked him the last time. I'm sure if he saw me again, he'd pass me by."

"Hitchhiking doesn't seem out of place here. In fact, it's part of the charm of the place. I've even done a little of it myself."

"What?" This is a new revelation. "You're kidding. When?"

"Well, during World War Two in Assam Valley, south of the Himalayas in China. I was stationed there in the Army Air Corps. I hitchhiked all over the place. After the war, I hitched a ride from North Carolina all the way back to New York City. And here is something crazy that I haven't thought about in forever."

"What's that?"

"When I stepped out of the subway in Brooklyn, I walked straight into my father, whom I had not seen in years."

"That's a crazy coincidence. Did you ever hitchhike up here in the Vineyard?"

"Yes, about ten years ago. The car was in the shop for a week, so it was the only practical way to get around. I found it easy to get a ride, and to be honest, I really enjoyed myself."

I think about this for a moment. "You were a seventy-five-year-old hitchhiker?"

"Yes."

Like father, like son. "So when I look at you, I see my future?" (Oh my God . . .)

"In more ways than one." He's probably right. "The apple never falls far from the tree."

"Dad, it's nice to finally talk."

He pats me on my leg. "It's funny, but telling you that story about running into my dad makes me realize that we have probably spoken more on this ride than I ever did with him."

"Really?"

"He and my mother could not get along, and the Depression only made matters worse. She rode him constantly about not making a living. It must have broken his heart. He left when I was pretty young, and I never saw him much after that." He shakes his head. "I remember so little about him." My dad gets a far-off look in his eye. "He was a gentle man. I never heard him raise his voice."

"I'm sorry." I feel like I just had the wind knocked out of me. Putting my hand on his arm, I say, "I appreciate everything you've done for me."

"We do the best we can."

The next few minutes pass in silence, as the smell of jasmine and sadness hangs in the humid air.

We finish up our errands, and he drops me in town. I kiss him on the cheek and whisper, "I love you, Dad."

He starts to pull away and then stops. "You should come out and see us. We miss you."

"I'll ride out soon. I've missed you, too. Give Mom my love. Oh, and thanks for the ride."

"You're welcome." He hands me an apple from a bag on the backseat. "Here, take this."

"In lieu of a dougÚut?"

He smiles. "It's good for you." This small act touches me. With that, Dad drives off, concluding our only one-on-one interaction of the summer.

It feels strange to come across my father so randomly. Though the two of us live within a mile of each other, we exist in parallel universes. I picture myself in his shoes: I'm near the end of my life, and my son is close by, yet I'm completely indifferent to his existence. I search my soul for empathy, but come up empty-handed.

It's hard to face, but it feels as though I don't really matter to my father.

I wander down to the waterfront and think about all the fathers I have been meeting lately, and the admirable qualities they seem to embody. Can I find things to admire within my own father?

A few observations bubble up within me. Dad may not be wealthy or famous, but he has integrity. He's always been a humble, stand-up kind of guy. And he's brilliant, with one of the sharpest minds I have ever encountered. He served in the United States Army Air Corps during the Second World War in exotic locales like India, Burma, and

China. Did he once have a great passion? Mom once mentioned that Dad had been the lead in all the school plays, and had considered pursuing an acting career in Hollywood.

What happened? What were his dreams?

The answers to these questions remain mysterious to me. It saddens me that I seem so incapable of reaching him.

As the fog creeps across the harbor, I hold the apple tentatively between my hands, and then slowly take a bite.

CHAPTER 24

Black and White

A few nights later, I am on a bench at the corner of Water Street and Main listening to the old minstrel Dave sing and play his guitar. More stylist than purist, he moves me with his unique interpretations of the classic and obscure.

Between tunes, he regales me with his theories on everything from the Illuminati to UFO abductions. "Have you seen the latest crop circles with the Fibonacci code in them?"

"I have not."

"Check it out; it will blow your mind." And with that he starts his second set. As the songs roll off his tongue, I watch the human genome parade stroll by. What a scene.

"Dave, this is truly the greatest show on earth." The people are out in droves, and they're not the only species walking the streets. The skunks are roaming about, too.

That's right, the skunks!

According to Vineyard legend, an island politician who was angry over a lost election decided to exact revenge on the locals. He introduced the creatures to the island (talk about the foul stench of politics!). Now the skunks are everywhere. I hold my breath as two of the creatures pass within a foot of me. Hey, who said humans and animals cannot coexist?

I turn to the man next to me and a few minutes into the conversation I realize it is Henry Louis Gates, the Harvard professor who recently gained fame when he was mistakenly arrested in his own home. (Believing Dr. Gates posed a threat, the police handcuffed him and carted him off. Later, in an effort to move race relations forward, President Obama invited Dr. Gates and the arresting officer to the White House for a groundbreaking photo op.)

Dr. Gates is charming, witty, and warm. He also limps severely, walks with a cane, and is very small in stature.

In the midst of our conversation, I inadvertently chuckle at the absurdity of this person posing a threat to anyone, let alone four large, armed police officers. When he looks at me strangely, I explain my laughter and add, "I think you handled your recent confrontation extremely well."

"Thank you. I appreciate that," he replies. "You should come to my racism symposium at the Whaling Church. We have a terrific panel this year."

"I'd love to." We say good-bye, and I watch him hobble off down Water Street.

The next morning at the Espresso, I have an idea. I could interview Dr. Gates about the evolution of race relations and have it published in the *Vineyard Gazette*. Five minutes later, fate lends a helping hand when my buddy Ben introduces me to Julia Wells, the paper's editor. (I love it when stuff like this happens!)

Julia agrees to print the piece if it lives up to the paper's lofty standards.

They depart, and I go back for a French roast refill. While waiting in line, I meet an interesting woman who informs me that this is her first visit to the Vineyard, so I help her with a few insider tips. I take my coffee out into the garden to plot my next move. The woman wanders out and asks, "May I join you?"

"Please."

Eventually we get around to introductions, and with typical island informality no last names are given. We share a fascinating conversation about her experiences as an activist and an artist. "When it comes to race, do you feel as a society we are evolving?"

"In some ways yes, and in some ways no. As an African American, I can tell you that we still have a long way to go."

"What type of work are you involved in?"

"I'm an actress. For a long time I was on the television show *ER*. Have you seen it?"

"No, I missed that one. So I am oblivious to your fame and misfortune."

She laughs. "I could tell. Interacting with a person who knows me based on celebrity is much different than someone approaching me cleanly. I prefer to meet someone who is unfamiliar with my work. Then, I feel like they're enjoying me for who I really am."

"Who said I was enjoying you?"

"You're funny."

"Not really. Though you should hear me sing. Do people usually recognize you?"

"All the time, and believe me, it gets old fast. Hey, I'd better go. It's my last day, and I have a ferry to catch."

I stand up. "It was an honor." She smiles and departs.

Just a few weeks ago, I overheard two middle-aged white guys talking about a black family walking by. "There sure are a lot of 'them' around town this year. I wish they'd all stay in Oak Bluffs where they belong."

I wanted to turn around and confront these Neanderthals, or at least throw some hot coffee on them, but what would be the point? I'm sure the guy had a bumper sticker on his truck that said PRACTICE RANDOM ACTS OF STUPIDITY.

How could people think this way? How did we devolve to a place where skin pigment is so important? Now, if someone acts like an asshole, that would matter, but their skin tone is irrelevant.

Maybe I'll never understand these things.

I decide to go down to the bakery and seek solace from the Sage. I greet the Sage and ask if he would like to join me next week at the racism forum.

"That sold out weeks ago," the ever-informed Sage replies. "You need a ticket to get in."

"Maybe we can crash it?"

He hands me a couple of cinnamon-sugar masterpieces. "Nah, that would be tacky. You'll have to surrender your fate to the ticket gods, and hope for the best."

That night I'm sitting on a bench in Edgartown when

my brother calls. We spend a few minutes catching up, and then he asks sarcastically, "Have you seen your friend Larry David lately?"

"Actually I haven't. Maybe he's already left the island."

I glance down the street, and lo and behold, who do you think is walking my way?

"Chris, I know you won't believe it, but I just looked up and Larry is walking straight toward me."

"No, he's not."

"I'm totally serious. Here he comes . . ."

"Hey, how's it going?" We shake hands.

"Great, Larry, and you?"

"I can't complain. Have a good night; I'll see you around." There is silence on the other end of the phone. Finally my brother says, "That is really weird."

"Yeah, it's certainly interesting. That reminds me, I promised to watch his show."

"Wait. You mean, after all of this you still haven't watched his stuff?"

"No. The weather's been so perfect. How are things with you?"

"Pretty good. I just got a part-time job teaching drama at one of the community colleges here in town."

"That's wonderful."

"It will be good to get busy."

The next day at the Harbor View Hotel, I meet an older man wearing a 2002 World Series championship ring. Given his imposing physique, I assume he's a former player. In the middle of our amiable chat, someone walks up and says to him, "I really love your acting."

"Oh, so you do a little acting on the side?" I ask.

He laughs and says, "No, the acting is my main thing. I've been in the field now for"—he thinks for a minute—"about forty years."

Uh-oh.

"In fact, one year I even won an Academy Award," he says with a wink.

I pause to ponder this, and then say somewhat sheepishly, "Ahhh . . . You won an Academy Award?"

"Yes. I won it for my work in the film *An Officer and a Gentleman*."

"And I call myself a film buff. I'm sorry, Louis, I didn't recognize you."

Louis has serious charisma, and I get the feeling, despite his age, that he could easily kick my sorry little didn't-even-know-it-was-Louis-Gossett-Junior ass. Fortunately for me, not once during our entire conversation does he get in my face and scream, *Don't eyeball me, boy!*

"Louis, didn't you start a nonprofit organization called *Eracism*?"

"Yes, I did, and I am really proud of that. I've been to South Africa and met with Nelson Mandela, and I also have a warm friendship with Archbishop Tutu."

"Do you think race relations are evolving?"

"Absolutely. But we still have an awful lot of work to do."

I say good-bye to Louis and then make a few detective calls to find out where Dr. Gates is staying. It turns out he is renting a home in Oak Bluffs, so I drop off a note with a request for an interview. Hoping that it might help matters,

I include a copy of my interview with the late, great columnist Carl Rowan.

I am working on a book called What Matters Most, *and hope to get an
interview with the prestigious columnist Carl Rowan. He served under
President Kennedy before going on to a distinguished career in journal-
ism, and in 1999 the National Press Club honored him with a Lifetime
Achievement Award.*

*Unfortunately, no matter how many times I try, Carl's assistant,
Pam, firmly replies, "I'm sorry, Mr. Rowan is just not interested."*

*One day, completely out of the blue, I feel a strong urge to pick up
the phone and call Carl's office. I try to ignore it, but it won't go away.
I finally relent and dial the number, fully expecting to hear Pam's familiar voice cordially blowing me off.*

Instead, this time a man comes on the line. "Hello?"

Startled, I scramble. "May I speak to . . . Mr. Rowan?"

A surly voice replies, "This is he."

*Oh my God, it's the Man. Stunned, I introduce myself and ex-
plain the nature of my request.*

*He listens politely before replying, "I'm sorry. I'm seventy-four
years old, and I'm feeling tired. I don't want to do any more interviews."*

*I press on. "But, Carl, I'm ready to get on a plane and fly all the
way to Maryland to find out what you believe matters most. Can't you
give me sixty minutes of your time? If not, quite honestly, you may not
be the kind of person who belongs in the book."*

*Holy sh-t! What did I just say? There is a deafening silence on the
other end of the line. Did he hang up? A few moments pass. "Hello?
Carl?"*

"I'm here . . . All right, I'll do it. Call Pam down at the office and tell her I said to set this up."

"Your office?"

Two weeks later, I'm sitting in Carl's living room, conducting our interview. Near the end of our long session, we come to a pivotal moment in his life. A sharecropper's son, Carl was the first person in his family to graduate from high school. He then went on to attend Tennessee State University in Nashville. After his first semester at TSU, he could not afford the twenty dollars required for the next term's tuition. So, defeated, Carl decided to return to the farm, his dream of a better life over.

As he walked through the bus station to catch a coach back to nowhere, something guided him. "Turn around and look on the ground. There, littered among the green transfer slips, will be the twenty dollars you need to continue your education." He hesitated, and the message came again. This time Carl went back, looked down, and sure enough, there was the money. Picking it up, he returned to college and went on to make history.

The world changed because of this small act.

"So, what do you make of this?" I ask.

"I know where you're going with this. You want me to say there's a divine plan or some deity made it all happen. What a load of horse crap! All I know is a person lost the money, and I was lucky enough to find it. Case closed."

"I'm not saying it magically appeared. But what 'guided' you to turn around and look down? How do you explain that?"

He looks stunned.

I repeat, "What guided you?"

His eyes dart back and forth as his mind searches for a practical answer. "Well, I suppose . . . It probably . . . I . . ." Then, like a small child, Carl stares directly into my eyes.

I gaze back.

Suddenly his tears burst forth. I reach over and take his hands in mine. He leans forward, weeping, and I put my arms around him.

A few months later, I pick up a paper and see the headline, LEGENDARY COLUMNIST CARL ROWAN DEAD AT 75. *Thank you, Carl.*

CHAPTER 25

Surreality

It's the day of the racism forum, and I still don't have tickets. I deal with my disappointment by riding to Chilmark on the back roads. I pedal past fields full of wildflowers, working farms, undisturbed ponds, and scenic overlooks. I smell jasmine and honeysuckle as the vibrant beauty of the Vineyard feeds me.

Reaching Beetlebung Corner in Chilmark, I have a decision to make: Do I ride farther to Aquinnah for a swim, or head back to Edgartown for the event, even though I don't have a ticket? With the temperature a brutal ninety-four degrees, the prospect of jumping in the ocean is a lot more appealing than that of sitting on a wooden pew listening to people discuss prejudice.

Cool comfort, or a scorching-hot topic? I decide to take a chance on the event, even though there's an excellent chance I may ride twenty miles just to stand outside in the heat, daydreaming about the ocean.

About halfway back to Edgartown, I pull into the West Tisbury Library for a pit stop. As I enter the building, Beth, the warm and welcoming librarian, is holding a poster promoting the forum. Pointing to the poster, I comment, "That looks like an interesting event."

"Are you planning to go?"

"I'd love to go, but it sold out weeks ago."

"Well, I have two tickets right here," she says, holding them up. "You're welcome to both of them. I was saving them for a good friend, but he just called me and said he's not going to use them."

"You have two tickets for me? Really, just like that?"

"Just like that." Beth hands me the tickets. "Please, be my guest."

"This feels surreal."

She smiles. "It all is. Enjoy the event."

Actually this isn't the first time a ticket has shown up out of the blue.

It's my twenty-fifth birthday, and my brother and I are making a pilgrimage to see Paul McCartney. His show is sold out and we are ticketless, but that doesn't dampen our spirits. We shall overcome.

Along the way, we travel back in our Beatles time machine. "Chris, do you remember as kids riding our bikes to Woolworth's to buy our first Beatles record?"

"Yes, and lying on the bedroom floor for hours listening . . ."

"To their masterpieces."

It occurs to us that we've been connected to their music for most of our lives.

We pull into a parking lot about a quarter mile from the arena. Before we are even out of the car, a guy approaches us and asks, "Do you guys need tickets?"

"Yes!"

"I have two in the tenth row. You can have them for half the face value."

Stunned, we accept. "Can you believe how easily we nailed that one?" I ask.

"This is so supposed to happen."

As we approach the venue, we notice the tickets have a date from months ago. Chris says, "We've been duped!"

"We should have been paying attention. That was naive of us, half-price tickets in the tenth row," I say, shaking my head. "Now what?"

"Should we throw them away?"

"No. Let's try to walk in and see what happens."

We casually wander over to the turnstile, trying to appear legit. The lady takes our tickets, examines them closely, and says, "You have fabulous seats near the stage. Enjoy the show." With this bit of news, our anticipation climbs to epic heights, and we go to claim our seats. We keep waiting for the real owners of these seats to show up, but they never do.

Before we know it, the former Beatle is in front of us, catapulting our goose bump meters off the charts. Near the end of the show, McCartney launches into his anthem, "Let It Be." Chris and I sway and sing along at the top of our lungs.

I turn to Chris and say, "This has to be one of the all-time highlights of my life."

"Absolutely. Definitely a top ten moment."

Leaving the library, I realize that I only have ninety minutes to bike ten miles, shower, and get me to the church on time. I call the Sage and exclaim, "I got two tickets to the forum!"

"Larry David?"

"No, Beth from the library. Meet me at the Whaling Church at five thirty."

I defy the laws of time and make it to the front door right before the program commences. With the Sage in tow, I collapse into a pew and begin to soak up the positive energy.

Our entertaining host, Dr. Gates, reflects on his recent tribulations with wisdom and humor. "I believe everything happens for a reason. It's important, when we are given lemons, that we make lemonade."

The theme of the event is "In light of an Obama presidency, have we reached a post-racial society?" I find the question absurd. As Martin Luther King Jr. once said, "Injustice anywhere is a threat to justice everywhere."

There is so much hatred and pain in the world, yet there also exists a great wellspring of love. We do face enormous challenges, but today we are gathering to try to address them.

This small act gives me hope.

CHAPTER 26

Invitations

I sit on the Harbor View porch savoring a cup of Colombian dark roast.

I begin to write in my journal when a woman asks, "Excuse me, would you mind watching my suitcase for a moment while I step inside the lobby?"

"Has the bag been in your possession the entire time, and did you pack it yourself?"

She laughs. "Is that a yes?"

"Of course. Take your time."

When she returns, she sits down next to me. "This place is so beautiful. It's my first time here, and I can't wait to come back."

"What brought you to the island?"

"I came to attend an event my boss was hosting."

I sense where this is going. "Really? Who's your boss?"

"Dr. Henry Gates."

I share my story about meeting Dr. Gates, the possible interview, the gift of the tickets, and my need to get in touch with him to follow up.

"Well, I have his e-mail," she says. "Let me give it to you."

What's going on here—does the island have a lottery? If it does, it's called *My Summer,* and I already won.

I walk down to the library and e-mail Dr. Gates a short note. Within five minutes, I receive a personal reply graciously declining my request. He plans to spend the remainder of his time on the Vineyard relaxing and recovering. Though tecÚically rejected, I feel no trace of disappointment; you can't win 'em all.

Perhaps in a subconscious effort to remain humble after my recent luck, I take a ride out to see my parents. It's been a while since I've been to The Parental Asylum, and after all, my dad said they'd like to see me.

Pedaling along the bike path, I try to imagine their level of excitement upon the return of their prodigal son—with a 1 being "Why the hell are you here?" and 10, "Look, honey, our boy has returned to us!"

My guess is it will be . . . probably around a 7, or maybe even an 8.

I enter the house. Drumroll, please . . . "Hello? Anybody home?"

No answer. I follow a low droning sound and find them sitting hypnotized in front of an old movie. It's *The Quiet Man*—the one filmed in Ireland with JoÚ Wayne. I know for a fact that they have seen it at least a dozen times, so the odds of their showing some enthusiasm for me are in my favor. This time, my presence will trump the dim blue light.

With gusto, I say, "Hello, Mom. Hi, Dad. I'm home!"

I wait for the excitement to kick in . . . Silence.

Still waiting . . . Nothing.

Okay, they're older. Let's give them a moment to warm up. Here we go . . .

Mom offers a quick, "Hi, son."

Dad looks up, says nothing, and returns his trancelike gaze to the screen. I reach down to pet Max.

"Don't hurt him."

I'm not ready to run the white flag up the pole yet. "How are you two?"

Nothing.

"Can I get anybody anything?"

The breeze blows through the house. The TV drones on.

"Anyone care for a walk?"

Refusing to surrender, I throw in a song and dance routine straight out of *A Chorus Line,* but it's no contest; the glowing box wins.

Parental Pilgrimage Epiphanies

- Got to experience the feeling of invisibility.

- Saw myself clearly as the Patron Saint of Hopeless Causes.

- Now understand why the TV replaced me in the family Christmas photo.

CHAPTER 27

The Prisoner of the United States

A few nights after my trek to my parents' house, to cheer myself up I duck into a trendy Edgartown restaurant with some friends. The place is packed. We grab a table and begin soaking up the festive ambience. While doing some reconnaissance, I notice a man with a familiar sheen to his head.

I have to go over. "Larry, my man!"

He greets me warmly and then announces to the group, "Hey, everyone, this is the hitchhiker!" His dinner party stirs with palpable excitement. "He's the guy I've been telling you about!"

It's obvious they know about our mysterious encounters, and based on their response I feel a little famous. "Larry, you're actually telling people about our nonsense?"

"Absolutely. It's too damn good not to!"

After a few minutes of small talk, we say good-bye and return to our respective universes.

The next day during another lunch on the porch at the Chilmark Store, a reporter from the *Gazette* randomly interviews me over the impending arrival of President Obama. (I secretly wonder if I am going to meet the president—will he pick me up hitchhiking?)

The paper is creating a special section about what Vineyarders, if given the chance, would say to Barack. Notebook in hand, he asks, "So, what would you say to the president of the United States?"

"Need any help?"

"Seriously."

I consider for a moment, and then respond. "Mr. President, I hope you have the courage to follow your convictions, and history will smile on those who not only have a vision, but take bold action. I believe our society has reached a critical state where only a new paradigm of consciousness can transform and save us. What I would like to ask you, Mr. President, if I may borrow from Gandhi: What can I, or any of us do, to *be* the change we wish to see in the world?"

When it's published the following week, I am disappointed to find that the last few lines were edited out.

Three days later, I'm riding my bike past the airport when a huge Marine Corps helicopter passes directly overhead. Instinctively I know that's him; that's the president. My next thought is more practical: *I hope I can get past security and up to the beach.*

Realizing that a vagabond on a bike is not much of a

threat, the police decide to let me through. I pedal past people holding homemade signs with endearing slogans who hope to get a fleeting glimpse of him. A few miles beyond the airport, I realize that over the last few minutes, not a single car has passed me in either direction.

He must be coming. Someone sound the trumpets.

Sure enough, within seconds, several state troopers on motorcycles fly past me. To avoid being squashed by the world's most elite motorcade, I begin pedaling furiously. An officer pulls up next to me and shouts, "Get off the road! The president is coming!"

God, if I only had a nickel for every time I've heard that one!

Just in time, I turn onto a narrow patch of grass and park, as a magnificent display of temporal power passes within a few feet of my humble bicycle. Instinctively I hold up my arm and extend the peace symbol, offering a small blessing to the motorcade. Isn't it interesting what a difference a finger or two can make in terms of message?

In an instant the VIP vortex passes, and calm returns to the scene. Though our lives pass within three feet of each other, our worlds could not be further apart. The birds sing on around me, oblivious to the famous life-form that has just flown by.

Imperial Impressions

- I feel like I've just witnessed the transfer of a prisoner.

- It must be limiting to constantly see the world through bulletproof glass.

- I'm in my ninth week here, while the Prisoner of the United States only gets a meager seven-day furlough.

- The imperial Prisoner of the United States has a lot less freedom than meaningless old me.

This is instantly illustrated when I ride a hundred yards and stop, without a care in the world, at a small lemonade stand run by a coterie of young girls. Could the prez do that without extensive planning? Or go nine weeks without wearing a coat or, heaven forbid, a tie? Can he walk freely among the people or casually eat a slice of pizza on the porch at the Chilmark Store? Could he lie on the beach at night alone, feeling at one with All That Is?

Most important, could he go hitchhiking and get picked up by Larry David?

CHAPTER 28

The Greatest Show on Earth

It's the middle of August, and my housing situation has come to an end. I look around for another place, but since it's the height of the season, nothing materializes. Maybe my run on the Vineyard is over. Hey, if I have to go, it's been a great ride. Instead of departing, I decide to tempt the fates and ask my parents if I can move back into The Parental Asylum.

I feel legitimately nervous as I make the two-mile sojourn out to my parents' habitat. Perhaps the old adage is true: *You can't ever go home again.*

Mom is in the kitchen as I enter and pop the question. "Mom, can I come home?"

"Of course you can come back. I would love it, and even Dad said he missed having you around."

"Thank you, Mom." I give her a hug and a kiss on the cheek.

"Can I make you an omelet?"

"Sure."

A portly Max comes up and nudges my mother's leg. "Oh look, the little man is letting me know he wants his breakfast."

"Mom, I think you already fed him."

"Nonsense." She goes on. "Aren't we lucky to have each other? To share this time? We are so blessed. These days, I feel happy just sipping my coffee or working in the garden. When you think about the big picture, it is all so miraculous."

I'm not exactly sure when it happened, but it's become apparent that my atheistic mother was abducted by aliens and then replaced with this deeply spiritual android. I would alert the proper authorities, but this replacement is so loving and kind, I don't have the heart.

Who is this person? The new Mom sounds more like a Himalayan monk than the woman who raised me. She doesn't seem to have a care in the world; how fortunate for her. Maybe we should all forget our unpleasant memories and live joyously. This form of ebullient amnesia would certainly help me.

"Mom, why are you always so welcoming to me?"

She looks out the window for a few moments, and I wonder if she's forgotten my question. But then she turns around, manages a slight smile, and sits down. "Well, when my older sister contracted polio, my mother had to make a choice. Only two of her three girls could stay, so I was sent away and raised by my great-grandmother."

I remember her telling this story, but I want to hear it again. "How old were you?"

"Ten. Part of me was relieved to get out of the house because my father was so cruel. He once knocked me out with his fist for wearing my hair a little differently."

"He hit you?"

"Right in the jaw. I was knocked out, and they took me to the hospital."

"Oh my God. I am so sorry."

"It's okay. That was a long time ago. I try to forget those things."

"After you moved out, how often did you see your mother?"

"She was supposed to come visit every Sunday, but many times she never even showed up. I used to sit for hours in front of my granny's large picture window watching for her car." Mom shakes her head. "I would wait and wait . . ." Her voice trails off.

Sitting across from my mom, I imagine that sweet young girl alone with her pain, and wonder if something inside her simply shut off. Feeling her heartache, I reach across the table and put my hand on top of hers. For a moment she gives me a loving look, the trace of a tear in the corner of her eye.

She looks off longingly into the distance . . . miles, or rather years, away. "That's why it was so hard when my mother was dying. I felt like I was struggling to find someone I always wanted to know. But once again I was left alone at that window, waiting for a ghost that never showed up."

She turns back toward me and looks me in the eye. "That's why *you* are welcome. A child can always come home."

"Thank you, Mom."

I move back home, and things are surprisingly harmonious. Believe it or not, I even manage to watch a little television with them. They seem to enjoy the courtroom shows, especially the one I call *Judge Yenta and the Trailer Park Court*. Each episode consists of participants apparently immune to humiliation, who stand in front of the well-lit Yenta arguing about life-and-death issues such as: He stole my cigarettes, she pawned my bong, they never paid back the bail money, she lost the remote, et cetera. Though I find the show fascinating, it's not nearly as entertaining as my parents' running commentary.

"She should have never let that bum move into the trailer. Not with that haircut and all those tattoos. He looks like trouble. Get a job, loser!"

Sensing an opportunity for some solidarity, I jump in. "Why does she have curlers in her hair? Where could she possibly be going later that is more important than being on national television right now?"

"Maybe she has a date," Mom suggests. "Stick around. This is a special one-hour episode."

Researchers say that the average person watches nine years of television in their lifetime, but I sometimes think my parents have decided to watch their combined eighteen years in one summer.

"No, thanks. I'm going to ride my bike up-island and take a swim."

Amid all this electronic jurisprudence, Max has been giving himself a head-to-toe cleaning. Max is a huge believer in the healing power of licking, though with what he is doing in this moment, he runs the risk of being arrested by the vice squad. I reach down to pet Max.

"Don't hurt him."

On my way to the beach, I drop into the Edgartown Stop & Shop, pick up a sandwich, and step into the check-out line to pay. The bagger asks, "Paper or plastic?"

"No, thank you. I don't need a bag."

She smiles. "Do you remember me?"

I give her a closer look and say, "The hat threw me, but I have to admit, the brown polyester really works for you." The homeless woman I met just a few weeks ago laughs and playfully slaps my arm. I look down at her name tag. "So it's Linda. How nice to finally put a name to your face."

"I'm doing much better, and I've even found a place to live."

Happily removing the word *homeless* from her description, I say, "Congratulations."

"Oh, and I've decided to stay on the island through the winter. They'll really need me in the off-season."

"We all do. Thanks for giving me hope."

"I gave *you* hope?" She tilts her head. "How?"

"When things improve for one of us, they improve for all of us. The whole world is a little better today because *you* are, and this gives me hope. There are no small acts."

"Ah, there you go again, talkin' all crazy."

"I told you I tend to ramble. Look, every day billions of things go right—people helping each other, random acts of kindness, bridges that work, flights that arrive—and yet none of it makes the news. All of these small acts make the world go around."

"Maybe you should be a preacher?"

"Am I that bad? I could use a job. Being a professional bodysurfer doesn't pay like it used to. Maybe I should fill out an application?"

She smiles again. "Get out of here."

"Take care of yourself, Linda."

As I turn to leave, she gently touches my arm. "I owe you this." She is holding a crumpled twenty-dollar bill.

"I knew you were good for it. But do me a favor." I place my hands around her hand with the money. "Find someone who needs it more than us and invest in them. It's your turn to pay it forward."

She looks down at our hands and then up at me. "I will."

For a moment our eyes meet. "See you around, Linda."

I take my lunch over to a bench in the park and think about Linda. How far does a person have to fall in their life for a job paying minimum wage to become a high point? Some children wander past me, their faces reflecting the joy of a bright summer day. Do any of them currently dream of someday becoming a store clerk? Or sitting behind a desk for hours on end concerned with menial things? What happens to a person who no longer has dreams?

An older man wanders up, eyes my sandwich, and says, "That looks good."

I ponder for a moment and then hand it to him. "Here, take it."

"Really?"

"I just had a sudden craving for pizza."

"Thank you."

I get back on my bike and head to Chilmark for my

daily slice of pizza. I grab a heavenly piece of pie and settle into a rocking chair. Three sparrows gather around my feet for any crumb I may be willing to part with. In between bites, I tear off bits of crust and scatter them for my winged friends.

A trio of boys around the age of ten cautiously makes their way over to me. I break the ice by asking, "How are you guys?" That's all the prompting they need, and they're off to the races. They proceed to give me their entire summer rundown in intricate detail.

Ten is such a wonderful age. These three are not concerned with the housing market or the politics down at the office. There's no stress over the state of their marriage. Life still seems full of infinite possibilities. The kids seem delighted to have (what appears to be) an adult giving them the time and attention they deserve. Later, I confide to them my secret: Though I may look older, on the inside I'm also ten years old.

"Just like Josh in the movie *Big*?" they ask.

"Exactly."

Eventually the boys depart, and I walk down to the beach, past a group of teenagers typing away on their handheld devices, while a few feet away one of the most gorgeous panoramic views imaginable invites adoration. When did we get so obsessed with these tiny screens?

A moment later, four lifeguards sprint past me toward a small crowd gathering along the shore. I watch as someone is pulled from the sea. I remember my own experience, and hope this person shares a similar outcome. When one of the lifeguards returns, I ask, "Is he going to be okay?"

"No, he didn't make it."

And just like that, another life comes to an end. A person's death seems out of place on such a spectacular day. The sun is shining brilliantly and the ocean appears to be no different, yet the world has changed. There is nothing like birth, death, and disaster to bring our priorities into alignment.

Who was this man? Did he have a family? When he woke up this morning, did this day seem any different? Did he have any plans for this evening? He came to the beach, went for a swim, and never made it out of the water.

I am reminded, once again, that all things must pass. Everything, everyone, all things will one day no longer be. We move like a shooting star through the ether of time. We have the capacity to hold this truth, which for some is crippling, while for others it is liberating. For me, it makes society's obsession with material things an interesting choice.

CHAPTER 29

Dancing with the Cosmos

Opening the door, I hear music playing and see two champagne glasses sitting by the fireplace. After checking around downstairs I walk up to the master bedroom. I enter the room to find the Miracle locked in a sultry embrace with another man. Confronted by my presence, the two of them start laughing . . .

I awake to see the Asylum's familiar walls.

Though I never left the safety of my bedroom, I feel destroyed, heartbroken, and in a terrible state of panic. It takes a while, but I finally calm down and stop hurting.

I begin to wonder: How is the suffering in my nightmare any different from the pain I have felt at different points of my life? The dream only hurt because I believed it to be real.

My longtime Nashville mentor, Nelson Andrews, a pillar of the community and founder of numerous organizations, is dying. His son calls to say, "Dad is not going to make it through the night. He wants to say good-bye to you and the Miracle."

Nelson, always a big fan of the Miracle, does not know of our dissolution. With his health failing, I don't have the heart to tell him.

Having not spoken to the Miracle lately, I am hesitant to contact her. The last couple of times we interacted were deeply painful, and I am in no hurry to feel that way again. Still, it would be selfish to deprive Nelson of a final good-bye, so I relent and call.

We meet outside his home. "How are you, Miracle?"

"I'm so sad about Nelson."

"Me too. He's been like a father to me. He's not even gone, and I already miss him."

His loving family is gathered around him, and I feel honored to be included in his inner circle. I recall our countless lunches, the constant support, phone calls that opened doors, and how this pillar of the community took an insignificant nobody like me under his wing. Mostly, I remember the things he modeled: a healthy family life, balance, service, and humility. Nelson taught not by telling, but by living.

Now here at the end, I kneel in front of him. We hold hands and look deeply into each other's eyes. "Nelson, thank you for everything. For all of the kindness, and for all of the wisdom."

With tubes running from his failing body, he musters the strength for a few wise words. "It was all stupidity, my friend." He is humble to the end. "I want to tell you something important." He points toward the Miracle, sitting by my side with tears in her eyes. "You need to hang on to her. You two have something special. Never let her go. Don't ever lose each other."

His words are like daggers in my chest. I drop my head and weep. After a few moments, I pull myself together and offer comfort to his longtime wife, the loyal and loving Sue.

She tears up and shakes her head. "Even after all these years, it never feels like enough time. You are always left wanting one more day."

I take Nelson's hands one last time. "Good-bye, my friend. You will be missed, although I'm sure I will see you again." I put my arms around his frail shoulders and try to seal his presence within me.

After a while, the Miracle and I depart. We silently embrace one last time, before reluctantly returning to the emptiness of our separate lives.

Lying there in the dark pondering all this, I remember an interesting story. Last spring my friend and I stood in his yard wondering why a huge walnut tree was dying. This seemed strange since all of the other nearby trees were in perfect health. He recalled standing next to the same tree a year earlier and saying to his wife, "When we build the swimming pool, we'll have to cut this walnut tree down."

If it's true that we create our experience, this story demonstrates what the quantum physicists call "the Observer Effect." This is where the observed phenomenon is influenced by what the observer expects. This fact has been proven scientifically, though I don't need to see the lab sheets to believe it.

I am living it.

I come to the painful conclusion that my relationship with the Miracle is the dead walnut tree in my neglected garden. Despite her loving efforts, I continually pushed her away. Because I did not believe in her or us, our relationship came to a slow and painful death—just like the walnut tree. It is time for me to own this difficult truth. With this realization comes the possibility for change, and a ray of hope for a new tomorrow.

Pondering this, I peacefully fall back asleep.

When I awake, it's as if a heavy weight has been lifted from my heart. I feel a sense of peace, and no longer carry a negative charge around my feelings for the Miracle.

That evening, after enjoying an ice cream cone, I begin to wander around the back streets of Edgartown. I suddenly notice a small, old cottage. Wait a minute; I know this place . . .

I'm twenty years old, and I'm playing the piano for a tiny woman named Mrs. Wuerth. She and I met through a mutual friend who happened to be her neighbor. In her late nineties, she has shrunken down to the size of one of those porcelain lawn jockeys. Fortunately for me, the size of her spirit stands in direct contrast with her diminutive form.

The two of us talk for hours, and no matter what the subject, she enthusiastically exclaims, "Isn't it wonderful?"

My flawed piano playing, my latest crush, the crushing blow, the bees pollinating her flowers, my presence, our friendship, the endless mysteries, the noble quest, impending death, the smell of babies . . . And she always rejoices, "Isn't it wonderful?"

I am much too young to know it, but she is right. Mrs. Wuerth, pronounced worth, *was perfectly named. She didn't know the price of anything, but Mrs. Wuerth knew the value of everything.*

The next summer I arrive and immediately ride my bike to her home. I come looking for reunion, but instead discover an empty house.

Sometime during the winter, Mrs. Wuerth passed away. My tiny friend with the huge heart is gone.

"Isn't it wonderful?"

Yes . . . but just a little less so than before.

Reveling in her memory, I walk down to the lighthouse and sit on the beach. I look up at the heavens and ask, "Must we always lose the ones we love?"

A shooting star crosses the horizon, and I think about Mrs. Wuerth, the Miracle, Nelson, and my father . . .

Dad's sister Claire has terminal cancer and is in a long, slow decline. She desperately wants to see her closest sibling one last time. Dad promises to come to New Jersey, but keeps putting it off. He just can't bring himself to face the buried skeletons of their past: the childhood deprivation, the absentee father, the collective suffering—it is simply too much.

He talks of seeing Claire, but one sad day it is too late, and she is gone. There is no good-bye, no closure, and no peace. Only grief.

Around this time Dad's mother is hospitalized for depression. She has been kept in the dark about her daughter's condition. The day after his sister dies, my father drives over to visit his mom. She surprises him by inquiring about Claire, feeling as if something is very wrong. He assures her that everything is fine, kisses her on the cheek, and promises to visit tomorrow.

That night in her sleep, his mother dies.

After the funerals, my father discovers that his remaining sister has stolen the inheritance intended for each of the grandchildren. When confronted, she offers to split the money with Dad, but deprive their nieces, who have recently buried their mother. Since this proposal is unacceptable, he implores his last surviving relative to do the right thing. She refuses, and my dad never speaks to her again.

In the span of a week, my dad loses his entire family.

I see a man frozen in shock who moves through the world like a zombie. When I ask him if he is okay, he stares back blankly and simply says, "Yes."

In the days that follow, Dad begins to shut down and withdraw from the world. At sixteen, I have no clue how to reach him. The decline is subtle and slow, like watching a ship sail farther and farther away, until a time comes when only the memory of the magnificent vessel remains.

So maybe that is what happened. My father's tragic predicament must have gotten lost in the limitations of my teenage egocentrism. Something in me shifts, and I see a man with faults, fears, disappointments, and pain. Just like me. With this realization comes an overwhelming sense of compassion and love. I think of my parents, and then I think of the Miracle.

I write their names in the sand next to words like PAIN, DISAPPOINTMENT, and BETRAYAL. My eyes well up, and tiny drops fall into the sand; tears of forgiveness.

A moment or two passes, and then a wave cascades over my grievances, returning the shoreline to its pristine condition. The next wave washes over and emancipates me. And then another . . .

Looking back over the summer and all the people who crossed my path, I find a common thread: We are all hopelessly human, simply doing the best we can with what little we have. My father, Bill, the blue bloods, the famous, the homeless, Dave, Birdman and Nancy, Mike and Doug. In the end, we all just want to belong and be loved.

I decide that come the morning, I will call the Miracle and try to find some peace with the regret I am carrying.

The time has come to reach out.

CHAPTER 30

Resonance and Reunion

It's early the next morning, and I am listening to the sound of the phone ringing in my ear. "Miracle, please pick up." Ring, ring, ring . . . "Pick it up . . ." This feels too important to leave a message.

"Hello?"

"Good morning. It's me."

"It's early. Are you okay?"

"I had to hear your voice." I share what I can of last night's experience under the stars, and then add, "I wish you could be here with me, and feel the magic of this place."

"Me too. Do you remember back in Del Mar when we talked about you showing me around the Vineyard?"

"Yes, of course." I begin to open my heart. "I don't feel like we've been apart this summer, because in a way you are always with me. You live just beneath the surface of everything I do. I've got to be honest: It haunts me that I never gave us my all. I keep asking myself, what would have happened if I had put us first, and loved you unguardedly?"

She begins to cry softly.

"I'm sorry, sweetheart."

"I miss you. I always miss you."

I realize that the time has come for me to cross the room, heart in hand, and once again ask her to dance. "Why don't you come to the Vineyard? I mean, I feel as though we aren't finished. That there is more to our story than this unhappy ending."

There is a long pause on the other end of the phone.

Will she step in my direction? Or once and for all, are we truly over? Does she have it in her heart to give me another chance? Or is it simply too late? I feel utterly vulnerable; there is so much at stake here.

I hear her breathing on the line.

I go for broke. "There's a line in *The Prophet:* 'The depth and connection of love is never truly known until the moment it is lost.' I feel that way with us. I've been there, lived there, and mourned there. Don't make me go back there."

"Oh, Paul."

"Do you remember that Rumi quote we loved? 'Out beyond ideas of right-doing and wrongdoing, there is a field—I will meet you there.' I believe that field is on this island. Meet me here."

"I will meet you there."

I cannot put my elation into words. It's as if some higher authority has granted me a pardon. Like every life, mine has circumstances that I wish had turned out differently. Lovers often pray for a second chance to go back and make wrong things right. This time, the prayer was answered.

For our reunion to occur, a few practical things have to fall into place. Where will we stay? The Asylum is not an option. I make some calls and check the real estate listings, but completely strike out. Since it's the end of August and the peak of the season, there's nothing to be found. I reluctantly let it go and hand it over to the gods of reunification.

That night at the Atlantic restaurant, I am attempting to explain the Larry David phenomenon to the Sage. "It's really strange; the whole thing feels like an episode of *The Twilight Zone*." A moment later, as if on cue, Larry enters, grabs a drink at the bar, spots me, and heads my way.

"Hi, Larry."

The Sage turns to Larry and says, "He was just talking about you."

"Things are kind of strange with us," Larry says. "It's like an episode of *The Twilight Zone*."

"That's what he just said!" The Sage stares at him.

Then I can't help myself. "You know Larry, if you keep this up, I'm going to have to get a restraining order."

This makes him laugh. "What a summer. I can't believe it's almost over."

We chat for a few minutes and then Larry begins to leave. He turns back to me with a mischievous look in his eye. "By the way, have you kept your promise and seen any of my stuff?"

I'm shocked. "You remembered that?"

"Of course I did. We had a deal."

"Come on, the weather's been perfect! I know you're not a nature guy, but I can't stay inside a dark room and watch endless hours of TV when the sun is shining. Even for your unparalleled comedic genius.

"Once I get home or, heaven forbid, the weather goes in the tank, I'll watch your show. You held up your end of the bargain, and I'll honor mine."

He points a playful finger at me. "Okay. But remember, you promised."

With that, Larry vanishes into the evening mist.

As I'm leaving the restaurant, I run into my friends Emily and Sam, whom I met at the Espresso. They invite me to go sailing with them in the morning.

The next day I arrive at the dock, coffee in hand, and scan the horizon for the couple. "There they are!"

Just as I'm saying hello, my cell phone rings, and it's the Miracle. "I have some bad news and some good news. I just got a wonderful new job offer."

"You did? Wow. What's the good news?"

"Very funny. But here's the bad part: The latest I can begin is a week from tomorrow."

"Oh." I feel my stomach tighten as the prospects for our reunion suddenly look bleak.

"So if I'm coming to the Vineyard, it has to happen this week. Have you had any luck finding a place?"

"Not yet. August is the height of the season, and the island is packed."

"Well, they want my answer on the job by five o'clock. I'm sorry. I so wanted to come."

So much for our romantic reunion. I am devastated.

I board the USS *Lovebird,* and we set sail for the open sea. Before we are even out of the harbor, Emily asks, "Is your Miracle coming to the Vineyard?"

"I'm working on it, but I need to find a place for us to stay."

"Really? We're staying at Sam's family home in town, and the house is huge. You two are welcome to use the entire upstairs for as long as you want."

I immediately dial the Miracle and break out the great news like a bottle of Dom Pérignon. Excited, she shifts into high gear and begins packing for her immediate pilgrimage north.

After a sleepless night, I am down at the ferry dock nervously awaiting her arrival. Since I have no idea how we will relate or what kind of chemistry we'll create, I try to approach her visit without expectations. I do know that no matter what happens, if we are tender and careful with each other, a lot of healing will take place.

As she steps off the boat, my heart leaps from my chest. I had forgotten how strikingly beautiful she is. We hug, and the power of our love floods over me. Her skin feels warm, and her hair is so soft against my face. Her heart is pounding; no wait, it's mine. In many ways, this is our first embrace. The feelings arrive in huge waves as I am immersed in the depth of our connection. I realize now that this bond has always been there.

With tears in our eyes, we finally let go.

"Miracle, I never thought we would have this chance again. Holding you still feels like coming home."

"I had forgotten what you feel like—what *us* feels like."

"Until this moment, I had no idea how much I missed you."

"I'm so glad I'm here."

"Me too."

Not all of our interactions are filled with smiles and laughter. There are also painful and raw talks. Anger and indignation arise, spiked with "How could you ever do that to me?" moments. We also listen, hear, affirm, own, apologize, and seek forgiveness. Which over the days and through healing tears is eventually given.

Although at times extremely challenging, we navigate through these discordant rapids to a harmonious place of resonance and reunion.

I recall the wise words shared with me throughout this summer, and begin to integrate them into our courtship. In my old selfish days it was all about me, and what I wanted. Now I consciously try to put the Miracle first. After all, why are her desires and dreams any less important than mine? I try to listen more and say less. (With mixed results. Okay, okay . . . this still needs a lot of work.)

Though we obviously share a deep and rich history, our relationship suddenly feels brand new. May the old "us" rest in peace. Something fresh and beautiful is being created. This nascent energy does not merely work; it thrives.

We spend several evenings at the Atlantic restaurant overlooking the Edgartown Harbor, where the wonderful maître d' Jaime treats us like royalty; our favorite wine is waiting on the table, the latest creation from the kitchen is brought forth to be sampled, and a rich dessert completes the feast. These dinners feel like the coronation of my summer.

In the midst of all this romance and felicity, I often pause to appreciate the fact that Miracle is actually here with me. So many times this summer the possibility of our reconnection seemed utterly impossible. Yet here we are holding hands, falling in love again.

I feel grateful to have the opportunity to right old wrongs, and to love more unconditionally.

The magic of the island softens us and provides a space in which to grow. We start each morning meandering through the back streets of Edgartown down to the Harbor View Hotel for coffee and conversation. Sitting on the porch, we hold hands and watch the boats sail out to sea.

"This whole island feels like the sound of children's laughter," she says. I must say that she has always had a unique way of putting things.

"So then New York City would feel like the sound of children whining?" I ask. She smiles and gives me a playful pat on the arm.

We spend the afternoons hanging out at the beach in Aquinnah, taking long walks past multicolored cliffs hundreds of feet high. The cliffs, etched over time by six glaciers, remain a sacred place for the island's original inhabitants, the Wampanoag Indian Tribe. We take the moist clay and cover ourselves from head to toe. The sun dries the adobe earth, creating a full-body mask and removing the toxins from our skin and hearts. Encased in clay, we swim in a deserted cove as the water washes our souls clean.

As the sun drifts into the sea, I realize that I have finally found someone who will watch the sunset with me. With an old wool blanket wrapped around us, we watch the afterglow fill the sky. We sit with our mouths agape at the brilliance of the changing colors. "I can see why you love it here," she says.

"This place has always felt like home to me. Like you do."

"Ah . . . I'm so grateful to be here." She puts her hand on top of mine. "Thank you."

"I think I finally understand the value of commitment. Love is a lot like nuclear power; if it's not protected in a safe container, it can be extremely harmful and dangerous.

"Love may be precious and healing, but it is also extremely powerful. So we need to safeguard our relationship consciously."

She puts her hands in mine. "I'm in."

"Me too."

"Miracle, would you be willing to move back in with me? I want to give it another try."

She hugs me, kisses my cheek, and says, "Yes!"

We decide that this thing called "us" can be rebuilt from the ruins of the past, and that the two of us can learn from our mistakes, grow stronger, and move forward as one. Together we venture forth on newborn legs, one tentative step at a time.

CHAPTER 31

The End of the Ride

My original two-week stay has now stretched into its eleventh week, and there is no denying the first smell of fall on the breeze. Autumn always turns me inward, making me nostalgic for the warm, carefree days of summer.

With the hope of celebrating my dad's eighty-fifth birthday, I once again extend my stay. A lavish dinner is planned, but Dad begs off with a stomachache. The celebration is postponed twice, and then canceled. On Dad's big day, the Miracle and I stop by. We discover him in front of, where else, the Dim Blue Light. I try to get his attention to wish him well, but Dad only says, "Can you move aside? You're blocking the screen."

How fitting. I humbly acquiesce and depart . . .

My father and I sit across from each other, each devouring a huge bowl of ice cream. I am twelve years old. The only sound in the room is of our spoons hitting the dish.

I look up, and our eyes meet. Usually my dad looks away when this happens, but not this time. His face is open and unguarded, and for some reason I don't see my father looking back at me. Instead I behold a child with soft brown eyes, longing to be loved.

We continue to gaze at each other, and I am overwhelmed with unconditional love. I have never looked upon another in this way, let alone my father.

For a timeless moment, my father allows me to look upon his soul.

Though my dad has always been close by, I realize that never until this moment have I truly seen him.

On the way back to our love nest, I realize that, while I long to connect with him on a deeper level, for now I must settle on proximity. Dad's struggle with intimacy does not necessarily signify a lack of caring. We love each other deeply, but are unable to share each other's preferences.

I tried to sit with him and watch the news—or as I like to call it, "What Went Wrong Today"—but the endlessly-talking-well-coiffed-heads drove me crazy. I look to find a shred of truth among the carnival barkers, but any sustained viewing leaves me intellectually emaciated. Why would he spend his precious time focused on all the insanity in the world and on television's constant message of fear and consumption?

When I ask Dad to watch the sunset, he declines. Dad

is not comfortable sitting with me on the beach, and I can't watch *Seinfeld* reruns. We are two peas in a pod. It's that rare kind of stalemate where both of the players lose.

Over the past thirty years, I have repeatedly tried to connect with my father. Most of the time, I have found the door closed. Yet every once in a while we share a moment so pure, it is well worth the years of rejection and pain. While there is life, there is hope—so I must always keep trying.

In the blink of an eye, my final days on the island drift by.

On my last Vineyard morning, I take the Miracle to the airport and place my house key in her hand, comforted by the thought that she will be there to hold me tonight.

I return to the Asylum, grab my bike, and take one long last ride beside the ocean. For a moment I wonder why I kept running into Larry this summer. What was that all about? Maybe this is only the beginning—although I hope my next book doesn't turn out to be *Camping with Larry David*.

Laughing, I scream to the wind, "Larry, where the hell are you? It's time for us to say good-bye!" But maybe he has already left the island.

Back at the Asylum, Dad is withdrawn and decides not to take the trip with us to the airport. I have failed to reach him this summer, at least on his terms, and this saddens me. We hug, and I tell him I love him. He stands in the doorway as I step outside. Turning around, I put my hand on his chest, look deep into his world-weary eyes, and say, "Please take care of yourself. I love you very much."

I back away, and he lets the screen door slowly close between us. For a moment he stands there looking at me. What is he thinking? Gazing at him, I lift my hand and place it on the screen. He slowly lifts his hand and puts it against mine. Now, with only a thin screen between us, we touch at last.

Détente.

"Good-bye, Dad."

On the ride to the airport, Mom and I hold hands. I share many inadequate platitudes, knowing they may well be forgotten before she returns home. In times like these, words are hopelessly inept. Yet they are all we have to bridge the gap between us.

When the boarding call comes, I hold on tightly and thank her again. Our eyes meet, and I burst into tears. I cry like a baby for all the pain endured by her, my dad, and me. "Good-bye, Mom."

"Good-bye, son."

Sadly I leave her and stand on the tarmac in the thick mist. Where is Humphrey Bogart when I need him? I realize that sometimes you have to dance between the raindrops.

Before I know it, we are off the ground, and I am in the air. My heart overflowing, the clouds parting and the sun breaking through, I look back through tears as my summer fades from view.

Epilogue

First things first: I honored my end of the Larry deal and watched *Curb Your Enthusiasm*. Not one, not two, not even ten episodes, but all six seasons. (Although not in one sitting.) I found it brilliant, and Larry is terrific. It's easy to see why the show is such a success. I have yet to watch *Seinfeld*. Maybe if Larry gives me another ride, I'll check it out.

Since leaving the island, the magic has continued.

One afternoon back at home in Nashville, while working on the Ted Danson chapter for this book, I got a strong craving for some grapefruit. So I took a break and wandered down to the Whole Foods Market. I picked up my bounty, headed for the checkout counter, turned the corner . . . and ran straight into Ted Danson. For a moment I stood there in shock. Was I hallucinating?

If this were the Vineyard, or even Los Angeles, it would merely be an amazing coincidence. But to see him here in Nashville? No way!

Ted was standing with his lovely wife, Mary. In my synchronistic stupor I made a complete fool of myself. (The more things change, the more they stay the same.) I didn't say anything unusually dumb, but I may have come off as just another crazed fan. Fortunately, after a few tense moments, they recognized me from the Vineyard, and we shared a few nice moments.

Of course, the following summer on my very first day back on the Vineyard, I ran right into Larry at the Chilmark Store, and we finally had that lunch.

Acknowledgments

Shortly after I began writing this book, my dear friend Peter Dergee moved in. After watching me hack away on the keyboard for days, he became interested in what I was doing. "Do you mind if I take a look at it? I've done a little editing in my time. Maybe I can help."

So I had the good fortune to have an in-house editor, and a gifted one at that. Peter put in countless hours. The book would be illegible without his contribution. Most important, he made what is usually a lonely process lots of fun. If this book were a film, Peter would be its producer.

The Miracle had a huge impact on my rewriting process, instinctively guiding me toward more of this and less of that. Thank you, dear one, and may your beautiful heart always guide you.

The Great Simmons gave me pages of constructive notes. So did my structure expert, Richard Morton. Jana

Stanfield had some great ideas and suggestions. Michael O. in Atlanta was a great proofreader. These wonderful people also helped raise the book bar: Jill Franks, Marie Bozzetti-Engstrom, Susan Fondren, and Dan Casey.

My parents have done an amazing job of putting up with me through the years, and have taught me so much about life. When I think of what they came from, I am in awe of the love they have been able to manifest. My brother, Chris, has been my oldest and most loyal friend for most of my life. He moves through the world with a kind heart and a gentle spirit, leaving a wake of smiling faces in his path. I am fortunate to call him my kin.

To my wonderful spiritual sister, Catherine Lott, I really appreciate how you are *always* there for me. Thank you, dear one.

Mr. Alan Brewer had faith in me and this work from Day One. Alan also introduced me to my amazing agent, Angela Rinaldi, who has repeatedly made the impossible happen. AR, it has been such a blessing to have you in my corner. Thank you.

A major bow to the wonderful and dedicated people at Gotham who took me under their wonderful wing and made this whole process a real joy. Thank you, Bill Shinker, Lauren Marino, Susan Barnes, and the gang.

A couple of super-talented gurus took the book to a much higher level: Leslie Wells and Benee Knauer. I appreciate you sharing your wisdom and gifts. I am deeply in your debt.

A special thank-you to my many friends who love me so unconditionally (in no particular order):

The Late Saint Jack, Neil Warren, Malcolm, Norm the Giver, The Mighty Cam, Petey, Lucy, Kevin Ansel, JoÚny G., Monte, Ma Bevins, Mostopiece, Dennis, Dan Maddox, David, James and Marybeth, Bonnie, Mo, Sammy O., Peter Friedman, Tony Santoluci, Billy Block, Tom-Lucas, and lastly my favorite crust-man and dog, Moses.

On the Vineyard: Rabbi Jim; Bill Bennett; Dr. Katz; Tony on 19th Street; Kevin, Ali, and Tim; Sam and Emily; Jaime and Eli at the Atlantic; Kevin and Barbara Butler; David and Rosalee McCullough; Andrew and Angela Brandt; Dudley and Russell; Tristan, Mark, and Ann Ide; Suzanne, Pat, and April.

Oh, and in case I forgot to say it at the time: "Larry, thanks for the ride."

LET ME KNOW WHAT YOU THINK:

mvyhitchhiker@gmail.com

Also . . .

Facebook: www.facebook.com/paul.s.dolman

Twitter: psdhitchhiker

Please visit my site: www.hitchhikingwithlarrydavid.com

And . . .

Become a member . . .

I would love to stay in touch.